Take

Mountain

Discovering the you that never dies

A 40-day guided retreat

MOYRA IRVING

© **Moyra Irving 2013**

Inspirational Storytellers Publishing
Tauranga, New Zealand

'Inspiring hearts all over the globe'

www.inspirationalstorytellers.com

Design: Tony & Lesley Bailey Lesley_bailey@ntlworld.com
Cover Art: Earth Watch 2, a painting by Moyra Irving

For my son, John-Patrick (Jeeps) -
who knows all this and more ...

Contents

Acknowledgements	vii
Reviews	ix
Preface	xv
Introduction	xxi

Return to the Mountain: A Soul's Journey

PART 1   Preparing for Retreat

Chapter 1	*Retreat: Picking up the thread of life*	9
Chapter 2	*The Wilderness Experience*	19
Chapter 3	*Planning your 40-day and 40-night Retreat*	29

PART 2   On Retreat

Chapter 4	*Arriving: The Pathway of Silence*	41
Chapter 5	*The Pathway of Self-Knowing*	61
Chapter 6	*The Pathway of Discipleship*	83
Chapter 7	*The Pathway of Service*	103
Chapter 8	*Departing: The Pathway of Love*	129
Chapter 9	*A Matter of Life and Death*	151
Appendix:	Useful Contacts, Resources and Recommended Reading	171

Acknowledgements

I would like to express my gratitude to all who have contributed to this book:
To Bob Biddulph whose presence echoes through its pages, and to Lyn Harvey who insisted that I write it - and refused to give up until I did; to Julian Middleton for his generosity, expertise and enlightening critiques, and for helping me to overcome my 'stage fright'; to John Beaumont for the layout and to Lesley and Tony Bailey for their magnificent design work and ability to interpret my vision.
Thanks too to Lynne Kirwan for allowing me to share her lovely quotation at the end of Chapter 7.

I am also indebted to those who have given up their time to read the initial draft of this book; I have learned much from their insightful comments. I hope these will be of interest as much to the reader as they are to me (see Reviews).
Finally, to Lynne Ralph, editor of Inspirational Storytellers, special thanks for her tireless encouragement and for liking my work enough to publish it!

Reviews

1. Take Me to the Mountain is a book to be savored and cherished by all true spiritual seekers. This gentle and compassionate guide to living life as a Soul is a work to be read again and again. It glows with the radiance of the author's soul, as she lovingly leads the reader into the spacious, timeless reality of the eternal Self where transformation occurs. Moyra Irving has distilled gems of wisdom from spiritual teachings and from her own experience into graceful, fluid, and deceptively simple language that carries seeds of illumination. Golden keys to spiritual growth reveal how suffering and anxiety can be transformed into catalysts for living a peaceful, purposeful life of service. Anyone who practices the guidance offered in this book can expect to come away more fully healed and more actively part of the planetary wave of evolution leading toward the birth of a new world.

Nancy Seifer, *Author: When the Soul Awakens: The Path to Spiritual Evolution and a New World Era*

2. Go on retreat in your own home with this practical and simple to follow guide; an hour a day is all it takes to change your life. It is packed with practical, real life advice and inspirational ideas on planning your retreat, from flasks to ear plugs. Moyra Irving has used her own experiences and knowledge to blast potential barriers out the water. This innovative book offers a 40 day retreat that can be split I to 5 mini eight day retreats. Each day of this retreat is mapped out for you with 40 separate messages, on everything from

contemplation to acceptance, from patience to mastery. Written in a clear, accessible style it offers advice and exercises as a means of learning the skills of mindfulness and meditation. An excellent manual for anyone who has ever wanted to experience a retreat, but without the funds or time to facilitate it. This book is a must buy for anyone trying to navigate the vagaries of modern life. So what are you waiting for? Buy Take Me to the Mountain and go on retreat NOW!

Dr Liz Boath, *Reader in Health, Faculty of Health Sciences, Staffordshire University, UK.*

3. Wonderful! You bring so much spirituality, wisdom and depth and you write very, very well. I love it! You are a shining star, lighting the way for others.

Jo Berry, *International Peace Ambassador Building Bridges for Peace*

4. Last year I became almost paralysed through fear and desperation over the health of my son. He had been unwell but, just when he and I both believed he was on the road to recovery, he suffered a relapse. This was an enormous shock to me. I was just beginning to believe that after two and a half years of undiagnosed and unexplained illness his life might just begin to return and he would be able to enjoy the type of life his friends and other 23 year olds enjoy. I was worried about his future, desperate for answers, appalled that NHS couldn't have cared less, and generally very sad that I was unable to improve his situation. Most of all I felt lonely and forlorn.

I sat one afternoon and read every one of Moyra Irving's Take Me to the Mountain 40 Guidance Cards and realised as I read, considered and contemplated the advice offered, that my mood and feelings had altered. I became less sad, less lonely, less desperate - in fact, I now felt able to cope with the situation. Reading the cards had lifted my spirits.

I remember one especially: 'Peace is only a thought away' (card number five). Peace and joy sit within each of us yet we have to take time out, detach from life's circumstances and dramas to remember this. Peace and joy energise and recharge us - put us in a place where we are able to cope with life's problems. So I told Moyra: "Hurry up - get the book out there!" And she has. The preface of the book alone will touch hearts; it brought tears to my eyes. Your words testify that you are truly committed to bringing the 'Kingdom of God' to earth. We all need help and guidance to empower us to have an authentic, joyful and peaceful journey on earth and Take Me to the Mountain provides just this.

Lyn Harvey *(Healer and therapist)*

5. When Moyra asked me to write a review for her book I was initially honoured but then instantly paralysed by the recurring thought - how can I possibly distil my love, respect and admiration for a remarkable woman and her tireless inspirational work in only a few lines?

I am beyond excited that Moyra has committed her genuine heartfelt wisdom and lifelong commitment to healing and spiritual growth to writing which will be an enduring testament, if one is needed, to her indefatigable spirit and inspiration to others. From running local free healing clinics and weekend retreats to setting up a charity with the aim to end world hunger, Moyra truly stands at the forefront of a new humanity.

This book will speak to the heart of all those who are ready to answer the call of the 'New Age' - a call to reconnect with that sacred eternal place that dwells within the heart of each and everyone of us, a place from which humanity can be healed and propelled forward. The view from the mountain beckons and the journey begins here!

Dawn Barrington *(Post-Graduate Certificate in Emotional Education)*

6. Beautiful - this book is bound to be a treasure. You present the information so clearly and thoughtfully - I felt more peaceful just reading the text! Great work!

Nancy Wait *(Author, actress and artist), New York*

7. Moyra, your writing is inspired, lovely, and will touch many lives. Peace, Stevie.

Stephen Kalinich *(Songwriter and poet), USA*

8. It's like you are speaking to me personally... you describe everything exactly as I've found it. Amazing to be reading this and, as always, with your kind, caring, non-judgemental and relaxed way of saying things ~ you immediately put your readers at ease. Thank you for being you and sharing with us all. It's great that you have had these experiences, but to have your gift for verbalising them so beautifully is precious.

Stephanie Moles *(Complementary therapist), Belfast, UK*

9. I am in love with this book: it's uplifting, comforting, straightforward and simply Divine. It's a real gem; many, many people need to read and work it. You say so much without bombarding us with complicated techniques or fancy spiritual stuff. It feels like a one-to-one teaching and makes the reader feel confident in your presence and not at all intimidated.
Your book also made me cry ...

Marilyn Lockett, State Registered Nurse

10. Your wonderful Take Me to the Mountain Guidance Card Messages have helped me enormously especially during some challenging times. Initially I was motivated to choose a card when I needed support, guidance or comfort. However I often use them daily now by asking 'what do I

need to know?" The card's message is sometimes instantly illuminating, but at other times the meaning is somewhat illusive and may not be revealed to me until several hours, days, weeks or even months have passed: yet I still feel a sense of reassurance that whatever I need to know will unfold. I've also found that over time the cards reveal more as I deepen and grow, and I therefore regard them as an interactive tool reflective of my own personal development. Even the images on the cards provide food for the soul and can be used as a focus to aid meditation. They always amaze me with their ability to reach the heart and soul of the matter! I love them and highly recommend them to anyone serious about knowing themselves better and deepening their appreciation and understanding of Life. Thank you so much.

Phil Warburton *State Registered Nurse*

11. Not even once have I used Moyra Irving's guidance cards without being confronted with what I needed to consider with regard to that moment's issue, question or dilemma. I have felt challenged, lovingly scolded, inspired, reminded and/or guided at any given moment. The wonder for me lies in the sweet combination of her channelling of higher wisdom and guidance together with excellent translation of that timeless wisdom into a language with which I immediately connect. I wouldn't be without her cards or now my copy of Take Me to the Mountain as I continue on my souls' journey.

Georgina McCafferty *Psychotherapist*

12. A remarkable work, conveying many spiritual truths with great simplicity and the authentic ring of personal experience. Guaranteed to prove both healing and redemptive.

Julian Middleton *Author & Astrologer*

Preface

'You must begin to prepare for old age.' My friend Bob lit a cigarette and squinted at me through the smoke.

I nodded vaguely. 'You mean move the bed downstairs?'

He ignored my flippancy. 'Apart from learning to live with your limitations, you have books to write. Your life story, for instance.'

What! I laughed but was secretly horrified. Limitations - I didn't like the sound of that at all. And old age – did I really want to be reminded of my own mortality, of The End (of this lifetime at least)? Bob had a way of unsettling people and I was unsettled now, faced with a fear that up till then I had always tried to escape from – my own demise.

And as for a life-story; what on earth could he mean? That sounded too much like self-indulgence to me.

However, Bob knew how I loved to write. I told him once of a novel I'd begun. It lies in a cupboard, unfinished like a piece of old knitting, and is taken out and worked on from time to time. Sometimes I unpick it a little, sometimes I allow it to grow and take shape a little more, but then it is hidden it away once more, a promise of future indulgence.

'But won't a novel do?' I pleaded. 'That could be a life story in disguise.'

Bob was a powerful healer and guide. He had an exceptional understanding of himself and others, helped by his ability to see, feel and interpret energy even at a distance. Trained at Stanstead Hall, the well known UK Spiritualist College, he might well have become a celebrated medium had he chosen to follow that particular route. Instead his real passion was healing and spiritual growth. He used to heal, he would say, with house bricks, breaking down resistance to healing and growth wherever he found it. For him, 'being compassionate' might have meant kicking you when you were down, quite literally in my experience! His love could warm hearts but equally burn away illusion. *His was a fiery love*. Perceptive, blunt, but always loving, he didn't mess about because there simply wasn't time. He knew he didn't have much longer with us.

'What I mean is this,' he said, patient for once and drawing slowly on his cigarette. 'The experiences you've had – and will continue to have – will be an inspiration for others. Get writing!'

So eventually I did. I began with a collection of short stories or modern day parables which, I'm pleased to say delighted my friend. He followed their development closely, and had a deep understanding of their messages, especially one – *The Girl Who Watched the Wind* – which I believe he identified with. One of the last public lectures he gave was called 'The Importance of Stories.'

In my enthusiasm I also began work on three books at once; this one, *Take Me to the Mountain*, and its sequel, *Fiery Love*. And yes, even the novel that has been taken out of the drawer and now is a little nearer completion.

Bob was a true disciple,[1] a man who sought to know himself better through self-reflection, study and service. Yes, he smoked (to dull the agony his body put him through) and he didn't have the healthiest of diets. Yet despite his pain he never missed his daily meditation. Nor did he forget to pray, and always for others. In fact, he may have heard your name mentioned only once but, detecting some need, would offer up a prayer for you. I saw him cure intractable depression and mend a broken heart in minutes. He was flawed, as we all are, but also incredibly wise.

As for me, I am just an ordinary person who has made enough mistakes to have gained a measure of wisdom. Therefore I offer these pages humbly, in the hope that they might ignite some spark of interest for those who seek to walk The Lighted Way.[2]

What exciting times we live in! Today is perhaps the most interesting time in the history of the world, when humanity is beginning to raise its gaze and look beyond the obvious and mundane. We stand on the brink of a new soul-aware civilisation. You and I now have an extraordinary opportunity to demonstrate our power as *living souls* and together change the world for the better.

I am certain that soon, in our own lifetimes perhaps, we will have irrefutable evidence that death is not The End. The work done by the Spiritualist Movement in the 1800s has since been developed along more scientific lines by a number of psychologists and doctors, those with an interest in out of body and near death experiences. Already a well documented collection of such experiences strongly suggests that our true identity is eternal and that we shall continue to live on, as we have always done, as *souls*. Imagine a time when human beings will no longer fear death, when all know for certain that consciousness cannot be obliterated! (see Chapter 9, *A Matter of Life and Death*).

My hope is that these pages, especially those devoted to Immortality, will bring a sense of reassurance to those who doubt that Life is eternal.

It was through the loss of my friend that I discovered this truth for myself. I also discovered how Silence – the very essence of retreat – allows us to identify with our undying self. Periods of silence in our busy lives create a necessary space in which our spirit can thrive. Through Silence we are guided along many pathways to eternity, ever upwards to the highest realization any human can have: **the knowledge that he or she is Divine - and therefore Deathless**. This is the ultimate purpose of retreat and something that is perfectly possible to achieve within the everyday living out of our lives. **'Take Me to the Mountain' is a retreat that will fit easily into any routine and will cost you nothing!**

So, to this end I invite you to enter into retreat with me right now. May you soon discover that death is not The End and may you also remember *who you are* and *why* you are here at this time. **Perhaps a thousand lifetimes have brought you and me to this point of readiness. The world now waits, as we become examples of what is not only possible, but now unstoppable; the blueprint for a New Humanity.**

---

[1] Disciple: from the Latin discipulus (pupil or one in training). Initially our spiritual training is directly from the soul; it is self initiated. In this sense, and for the purposes of this book, a disciple might loosely be called one who follows the light of the soul. Some think of disciples as blind followers of a guru. This is far from the truth. A disciple willingly follows a path, offered to him or her by the activity of their own soul. Only then can he or she be trusted to work with the Elders of the Race, Those Who through a long evolution of consciousness have achieved mastery of Themselves.

[2] The Lighted Way: that which leads us back to our Divine Source.

Introduction

Forget all that you have been taught about God. Until you have knelt at your own altar in stillness and reverence you have not found Me. (Fiery Love: Message no. 20)

*T*ake Me to the Mountain is a retreat with a difference. Firstly, there is no place to escape to – no ashram, spa or secluded location. It happens wherever you happen to be.

There are no austere or complicated practices required - no fasting, no deprivation - and the whole experience can be fitted in to any routine.

It is simply a way of life; an everyday retreat. More than anything it is to be enjoyed.

The full retreat lasts for 40 days and 40 nights[1] but this can be divided into 5 smaller retreats of 8 days. It involves an inner journey to the Mountain – our 'High Place,' and takes in 5 Pathways. You will take one Pathway at a time for each one leads into the other and to the Mountain itself.

Retreat offers us ways to be strong and solid and calm in a world that may not be perfect; a world where there is too little time, too little money, where you hate your job - or worse, you don't have one; where you feel lonely and unloved. Above all it will give you a deeper sense of your Self, and resources that you never dreamed you had. Whether we call this 'Self' spirit or soul is really not important but for the purposes of this book I shall refer to it as both Soul and the Undying You. This is the aspect of you and me that lives beyond time, in a 'Now' that is forever. In retreat we have access to this timeless and Undying Self.

Retreat and the Call of the Soul
The Undying Self is our most intimate experience of God. You know how it is when you are captivated by a beautiful piece of music or a breath-taking view; or the sense of union with a loved one? In those moments of deep silence when time stands still (sometimes called a 'peak experience')[1] we hear our Soul (or personal God) calling. *Take Me to the Mountain* is a companion for those who have heard, however fleetingly, that Call. It may be distant at first, a mere whisper, but will inevitably gain your attention and become the great guiding force in your life.

It is then that the centre of focus shifts from 'me' to 'us' and we discover a greater interest in the wider world. We begin to see everyone and everything as an extension of our self and develop a greater respect for all living beings including the Earth, our home. We identify with one another with increased empathy and compassion. Our consciousness expands.

Consciousness
Divine intelligence or consciousness is to be found everywhere, within every living form: in humanity, in animals, plants and the mineral kingdom too. In human beings this consciousness or soul has evolved to the point of *self*-awareness - we have an 'awareness of awareness itself' together with the ability to reflect, and project. Because of this developed sensitivity most human beings will sense their soul as 'conscience' (*con-science* or 'with knowledge'), that wise but sometimes inconvenient faculty that steers us from selfishness towards the 'good, the beautiful and the true.' These qualities are the hallmarks of a truly evolved human being. When we are in tune with our soul we are more aware of our relationship with others. The principle 'Do unto others what you would have them do to you' is deeply imbedded in our consciousness and shared by every world religion and spiritual philosophy. It expresses the greatest of all spiritual laws, Love.

The God-in-Us

Without this Love Nature you and I, as personalities, would simply cease to exist for it is the very element that animates us, the spark of Life within, the God-in-Us.

The dictum 'as above, so below' proposes that all life forms are reflections of something greater, ultimately of the source of creation itself. This is something that many of us have always instinctively recognised as true. According to the Ageless Wisdom,[2] our soul is a reflection of an individual spark of God (Monad), which in turn is an expression of Divine Source Itself. Like everything else in creation, the smaller and the greater, our soul evolves until it reflects more perfectly the nature of its source.

To this end, we are told our soul creates a physical reflection of itself (a body, a personality). Over countless lifetimes each successive form it inhabits becomes a little more refined in its nature and therefore better able to express the soul's qualities.

One Life, Many Lifetimes

All this gives us a rather different perspective on life and death for evolution of consciousness is a very long journey indeed. It suggests that we have one continuous Life but many, many lifetimes within it. It also explains the Law of Rebirth (or Reincarnation). As individual sparks of God each one of us is divine and our ultimate purpose is to demonstrate that divinity, through trial and error in the ordinary living out of our lives.

The soul on its own plane of existence lives in an eternal state of bliss. By contrast, its temporary experience in physical form is both limiting and confusing. Yet without the soul's involvement in the world (a process called *involution*), it has no opportunity to learn and thereby evolve. **We are after all spiritual beings having a human experience**! (I have included 'Return to the Mountain' at the end of this introduction, a story that follows the soul's journey into matter and its eventual return to God).

Artist and esoteric author Benjamin Creme sums this up in

his article 'The Process of Evolution': *Rebirth is a process which allows God, through an agent — ourselves — to bring Itself down to Its polar opposite – matter - in order to bring that matter back into Itself, totally imbued with Its nature.*[3]

How then can death be feared if it does not herald The End but offers instead the opportunity for new life, new experiences and a new phase in our development?

Retreat: Our Return Home

As we evolve from lifetime to lifetime we are instinctively drawn to the Undying Life within us. Through various forms of meditation, mindfulness, prayer or silent-sitting we ultimately find the Temple within and learn to kneel at our own altar. **It is here we find our personal God**.

Humanity, having sunk to the very depths of materialism, is now in desperate need of a return to its Soul. *Take Me to the Mountain* is a guide for those who are ready to make this journey, consciously, and whilst living and working in the world. Our challenge today is to recognise the spiritual in everything and everyone and to know that to grow spiritually there is actually no need to be anywhere other than where you are now - for *the spiritual path is your own life*.

Retreat is not an escape but a return home, to the 'you that never dies.' It offers a gentle way of coming to terms with change and adapting to new circumstances, especially the transition we call death. It enables us to become strong and stable in times of uncertainty.

Retreat is both a gift to your self and to others. It will reduce your levels of stress and make you feel better. It will also make you a much nicer person to live with!

We shall begin by considering suffering as a catalyst for this return home, and the *Wilderness Experience* that may first inspire us to 'take refuge.'

Next we'll explore, step by step, 5 *Pathways to Immortality*. As already explained the complete 40 day retreat may be split into 5 shorter 'mini retreats' but whether you choose the longer or shorter version the aim will be to cultivate an 'attitude of retreat' throughout your daily life. Guidance in the form of the 40 messages will support you during this time, together with exercises and short meditations to accompany them.

Messages from the Mountain

This collection of messages emerged from my own initial retreat while living and working in the world. Guidance came in the form of a 'dictated' comment on a particular theme, sometimes personal but often more global in its nature. Occasionally it was light-hearted and even humorous, reminding me that spiritual doesn't always mean solemn!

The messages became (and continue to be) the basis of a period of personal training. These and others were later used for two sets of Guidance Cards (*Take Me to the Mountain and Fiery Love*)[4] and a series of guided retreats: *Take Me to the Mountain, The Blessing of Uncertainty, The Lighted Way, Fiery Love, Healing in Body, Mind and Spirit (Parts 1 and 2), A Matter of Life and Death* and most recently, *Discovering Immortality*.

Although the messages are used here in sequence, they may also be chosen at random or according to a particular theme that you are currently working with. If you have a companion set of *Take Me to the Mountain* cards you may also use a simple 'divination spread' of cards to represent past, present and future situations.

I have used the Guidance Cards many times over now and each time brings me a much deeper understanding of their meaning.

A Guiding Light

In one sense all writing can be said to be 'channelled', whether from the creative imagination or from some higher source of inspiration. Often this higher source is the writer's own soul, sometimes a teacher or guide on the astral planes (or simply the product of an over-active astral imagination!). In very rare cases indeed it is a Master Himself. As the controversial guru, Osho, reminded us: *Countless people are deceived by their own unconscious into believing that they are mediums of great souls or gods.*

So, being very wary of 'channelled guidance' myself, I am now in the unusual position of offering my own to you. I do this with no claim to its authorship, although this is not to diminish its value in any way. I ask only that you draw your own conclusions and take from the messages whatever you may find useful.

Finally, to their source I offer my gratitude for its Guiding Light. My own life has been inspired by it and my hope is that yours will be too.

Moyra Irving
November 2012

---

[1] 'Peak experience,' as described by psychologist Abraham Maslow: *Sudden feelings of intense happiness and well-being, wonder and awe, and possibly also involving an awareness of transcendental unity or knowledge of higher truth.*

[2] The Ageless Wisdom: a collection of spiritual teachings passed down through the ages and covering the origins and evolution of Life and the Laws that govern it.

[3] Benjamin Creme: *The Process of Evolution* (*Share International* magazine archives).

[4] Available through the Inspirational Storytellers website:
inspirationalstorytellers.com

Return to the Mountain:
A Soul's Journey

Above the highest peak of the highest range of mountains in the world, somewhere beyond Heaven and Earth, dusk falls and a lone star appears in an amethyst sky. This peak is not known to many and has been climbed by fewer still. Yet here, somewhere beyond Heaven and Earth, is a State called Perfect Peace. Here, beyond the seasons and the tides, young souls slumber and sing to the stars. You may sometimes hear their distant song.

Now and again a visitor called Time enters the remote State of Perfect Peace and awakens one from his dreams. He is looking for those who will travel with him into the Dark Unknown that stretches far below Perfect Peace. Now and again, and not realizing the sacrifice he is about to make, a young soul offers himself and, carrying only a bright lamp in his heart, he leaves the State of Perfect Peace to journey with Time into the Dark Unknown..

'Young Soul,' Time announces, 'always remember who you are! Your mission is this: to bring Light to the world below us.'

The way down is long but, guided by the light in the young soul's heart, they come at last to a high peak of great beauty and peace and capped with snow. The young soul hesitates here for a while, reminded suddenly of home. Then, surveying the valleys and river beds below them, all shrouded in mist, he and Time make their final descent. At last, after many miles, they reach their journey's end and unaccustomed to the darkness, the young soul blinks and rubs his eyes. He gazes, intrigued by his new surroundings.

A great hooting and clanging echoes around them; he winces, covering his ears. How strange is this noisy world with its curious forms and slanting shadows, and so far from

Perfect Peace! Already the snow covered peak is a distant dream.

'Where shall I take my light first?' he says, playing his lamp on rocky outcrops and tunnelling the crystal depths. He rides the wind on eagles' wings and sails to the silent waters of ocean caves. At night he sleeps beneath the desert sand and watches sunrise through the eye of a jungle cat. Deeper and deeper into the World of Shadow and Form the young soul casts his light until ….

Time passes by one night and whispers into his dreams: 'Young Soul, always remember who you are!'' But, so happy to play in Shadow and Form, Soul is already forgetting who he is. 'I am the dragonfly,' he cries, 'I am the snowflake, the mountain and the fire!' He leaps from one form to the next, dancing in the light of his heart, dancing in his own shadow, until finally he announces: 'I am Man!' And, as night falls once more in the World of Shadow and Form, the young soul's light slips deep into the heart of Man.

Aeons pass in the World of Shadow and Form and the soul grows weary as one mortal lifetime ends and another begins. 'Where has Time gone?' he will sometimes say as a great longing for something half-remembered stirs in his heart. 'Where can I find Peace, Perfect Peace?'

But, as the longing grows, so does his light, still buried deep in the heart of form.

One day his longing leads him to a place high above the World of Shadow and Form, where he can just make out the distant peaks of somewhere long forgotten. From his high place it is as though he sees, through the mists, his own Life unfold, lifetime after lifetime, and following comes a procession of memories, of pleasures and pain walking as partners, side by side in the valley below. But although he recognizes these memories as his own they now seem to be no longer part of him. He watches for a long time as thoughts come and thoughts go until finally echoes of a distant song appear. And suddenly, from his high place he sees the peaks of that somewhere long forgotten, and there is one final thought. Peace! The procession has halted now. Then sighing, he knows at once that Peace, Perfect Peace really is only a thought away.

He continues to climb until, as dusk falls, the distant song grows louder and the first star appears in an amethyst sky. Lifting his gaze, the mountains are no longer so far away. 'Is it Time?' he wonders and the light in his heart flickers and flares as, slowly, he begins to remember who he is. And at once a thousand other lights wink back – and more – until the whole World of Shadow and Form is ablaze with light. Then, hearing a familiar voice on the breeze, the old soul smiles as Time draws near.

'Are you ready for the journey, old Soul?' Time asks.

But ahead of Time Soul has begun to sing to the stars once more and, carried on a dream, he is already home.

© Moyra Irving 2006

Part 1
Preparing for Retreat

Chapter 1
Retreat: Picking up the thread of life

The secret is just this: you're always home, no matter where you are, because Now is home. Now is forever ...

When we were children we understood about retreat. We knew how to live in the moment which is really what retreat is after all. Watch any child at play and see how totally absorbed he is. Nothing else matters, not what happened yesterday or might happen tomorrow, just Now. He is focused in a world of his own imagination, unconcerned with what happened last week or what might happen next.

As a child it never occurred to me that I was young. I was just 'me,' exactly the same 'me' that lives on today and who has lived throughout time. I was also aware of a 'before life' (uncomfortably so at times) and reasoned that there must therefore be an 'after life' too – in other words some continuity of consciousness that exists beyond birth and death. Life was an ever-unfolding miracle, inseparable from the Now.

Some years ago I wrote a short story called *Now is Forever*. It focuses on two children who experience 'Now' as their true home and thus discover the eternal thread that runs through life. I wanted to experience a lost world through these two children, to re-capture the magic of childhood and show how this magic disappears once we grow older and life's challenges and responsibilities take over. I believe if we choose to, we can learn to be children once more and regain our youthful spirit. We can pick up the thread of Life again and find that 'Now' really is forever, in one single unending moment.

Children love stories that remind them of the magic that exists just beyond our physical sight. They are very close to the subtle worlds and will often know instinctively that beyond the physical there are countless 'worlds within worlds,' both the microcosm and the macrocosm. I was lucky; my father, a very stern man with a military background, was also of Irish descent and unusually sensitive. He taught me about the 'Little People' and I was able to 'see' fairies and not just read about them in books.

My son, I discovered quite by chance, was able to see auras and he naturally assumed that everyone did! His reading of other people was uncannily accurate. He, like many others, would often talk to unseen friends and also showed signs of remembering a 'before life.' He lost these psychic abilities for a while along with a degree of telepathy once puberty began but I think this may have been necessary for his development along other lines.

Left to their own devices – and under the right circumstances – children will naturally display other soul qualities such as empathy and the desire to help one another. Something else that is all too sadly lost later in life.

Retreat allows us the space to regain a child-like a sense of the timeless, and to see the world anew. This truly is living the life of the Soul.

Who Am I? Why Am I Here?

The more time you spend in the company of your Soul, such as on retreat, the more interesting life becomes. You may begin to feel younger, more energetic, because the soul is eternally youthful. You will inevitably start to identify with the timeless in you and lose any fear of death because you know you are eternal and therefore deathless.

You begin to search more deeply for meaning and ask questions, like *Who am I? Why am I here?* For every answer you find there is another question that probes more deeply.

When I was in my early teens I would search my local library for books that might reveal to me the secrets of Life. I knew that such books must exist but had no idea where to locate them. This was the pre-Beatles era, before meditation became popular in the West. There were no esoteric sections in bookshops or Mind, Body and Spirit Fairs, no computers to help me with my search. Then one day I happened upon a very old volume tucked away in the library's Philosophy section. I remember my excitement, reading about the 'Music of the Spheres' and although it made little sense to me, it was a start! A few years later I met a young man who belonged to the Rosicrucian Order, a modern-day version of the ancient mystery school. He taught me about meditation and so much more besides concerning the spiritual Laws of Life.

Today there are countless books on Eastern and Western spiritual philosophies; New Age publications abound. The problem nowadays is perhaps too much choice – too many cul de sacs and false pathways for the spiritual seeker to become lost in.

Enlightenment and Spiritual Ambition

My friend Bob often joked that all spiritual books should carry a health warning. He complained that too many made exaggerated promises of health and happiness and that some were positively dangerous. He had learned the hard way, sending himself half mad as a result of practicing certain unsupervised techniques. Spiritual ambition can have devastating results.

Most dangerous of all are those teachers claiming to offer 'enlightenment.' Any extreme exercises designed to speed up spiritual awakening (such as the forced raising of kundalini energy through breathing exercises) should, in my opinion, be avoided unless under the supervision of a highly experienced teacher. Kundalini (the dormant force at the base of the spine) is intended to rise through the energy centres normally and systematically and in its own time. Likewise, spiritual growth is best attained through a natural unfolding, facilitated by simple, tried and tested exercises, and always combined with some service activity. **To be in a rush to gain enlightenment (which is a never-ending process after all) suggests spiritual ambition - a contradiction in terms if ever there was one**!

Retreat, Meditation and Altered States

Retreat, meditation and a more relaxed attitude to life all lower stress levels and produce definite health benefits. These include lowered heart rate and blood pressure, improved digestion, healthier hormone levels and even increased immunity and fertility. There are many studies to support these claims, including Dr Herbert Benson's well known work 'The Relaxation Response.'[1] In meditation brain rhythms change from beta (active conscious) to alpha (rested and reflective), and also theta states (meditative and creative). Meditation therefore can stimulate memory and creativity.

Retreat involves periods of 'silent sitting' (meditation) and mindful activity. Any focused meditation strengthens our contact with our soul. This doesn't mean making the mind go blank but rather quieting the mind so that thoughts no longer disturb the inner peace. The actual experience of meditation doesn't matter at all. Sometimes it may be blissful, sometimes tiring or even downright boring! It is, I believe, the willingness to meet ourselves in Silence that matters most. Although meditation is an 'altered state' – that is to say it differs from ordinary waking consciousness – it is a most natural human activity.

There are said to be as many types of meditation as there are people and techniques such as mantras or breathing exercises are simply tools to still the chattering mind and help the individual to experience his own unique essence.

This practice of 'stilling' allows us rest in body and mind and leads ultimately to transcendence, a bodiless, deathless state.

People who have 'near death' or 'out of body' experiences (NDEs or OBEs) frequently describe the bliss and freedom of their bodiless state. In fact, the experience can be so compelling that they are reluctant to return to the body and may take some persuasion before agreeing to. In the extra-physical state worldly attachments no longer seem to have the same attraction – not even those people we love the most – in comparison with the ecstasy experienced there. Re-entry to the body is often reported as uncomfortable and constricting, although any pain felt on return is frequently transformed and redeemed by a new sense of perspective and hope – and even physical healing. There are many dramatic reports of cures following NDEs. Especially impressive is Anita Moorjani's account of her own return from death and recovery from terminal illness in her book, *Dying to be Me*.[2] (See Chapter 9, *A Matter of Life and Death*)

Many people discover their essential 'self' through spiritual healing – and this is the primary purpose of healing of course, to bring us into contact with our own Healer, the Soul. Perfect health and happiness can never be guaranteed although a state of contentment, even bliss, is certainly possible. It should be remembered though that any focused spiritual practice, while enormously helpful for our mental, emotional and physical health, also brings to the surface any unresolved issues we have. And we all do! In *Transcendental Meditation* this process is called 'un-stressing' and although beneficial it can be temporarily uncomfortable too!

Retreat and the release of stress

We often avoid silence and stillness for very good reason. Instinctively we know that without our usual distractions –

television, telephone, the internet, and so on – we are alone with our thoughts. Retreat can be both a refuge and a catalyst for the release of trauma.

It is in stillness that painful memories or unresolved issues arise, usually as tears or an outburst of anger. This process is a normal and necessary movement of emotional energy that is all part of the healing process. It can happen during private and public retreats alike - occasionally during my own. When it does I ask everyone to breathe with the person involved – as an example let's call him Joe. This breathing together results in a tremendous sense of being 'held' and supported. There may be a tendency to rush forward to help Joe, to console, but it is far better to allow him space for the energy to move off in its own time. Such a movement of energy can have a powerful effect on the rest of us and remind us of our own emotional pain. Our throats may tighten up, tears well up in empathy. I ask everyone then to continue to breathe steadily and to remain very poised. It helps enormously to raise the attention to our 'High Place,'[3] the Ajna centre between the eyebrows, and thus allow the process to complete.

People naturally feel embarrassed at having drawn attention to themselves so at some point I thank Joe for staying with it and for enabling us all to acknowledge our own pain. It all adds to a great sense of group coherence and bonding.

I Am the Mountain

At such times I have found it very helpful to identify with the mountain, solid and strong, eternally unmoved by winds and storms (see Chapter 4). This is a very simple technique: simply imagine your feet as the base of a mountain, your head as the summit and your whole body rock-solid and poised against any internal or external force. At the same time you think: *I Am the Mountain!*

The Messages included in this book often refer to mountains – how their peaks are not really as distant as we might imagine since we have already come a very long way through life's challenges, each one a mountain to conquer. As the famous explorer and mountaineer, Sir Edmund Hillary said: *It is not the mountain we conquer, but ourselves.*

So many of our difficulties are self-created, that is to say by the way we think. Indeed we are capable of breaking our own hearts by repeated 'wrong thinking.' Our obsessions and anxieties mount up over our lifetimes, yet this mountain of suffering is not as solid as we might imagine. It can be reduced to dust once we penetrate those layers with the light of awareness, the Soul.

The mountains and other remote places in the world have long been known as the retreats of the Masters, Those wise teachers who have evolved ahead of us and mastered all aspects of life on this planet – body, mind, and emotions – and now guide humanity from age to age. Climbing the mountain is an obvious metaphor for human aspiration; of our evolutionary impulse to reach towards some greater goal, to overcome our earthly limitations and so master ourselves. Self-mastery, whether or not we are aware of it, is our ultimate goal for we are all Masters in training.

Enlightenment and the Upward Struggle

Pain and suffering, as the Tibetan Master Djwhal Khul describes, is our *upward struggle through matter*.[4] It is only by enduring and overcoming those things we find most difficult that we eventually reach *the summit of the mountain*.

However, we would do well to remember that there are always further experiences ahead of us – yes, even for the Masters themselves – and greater summits too. That is the nature of evolution: enlightenment is only relative after all!

Retreat: The Blessing of Suffering and Change

Those who live with chronic physical pain often say that the worst kind of pain is emotional, especially the agony of loneliness, anxiety and depression. My wise friend Bob knew this all too well. Although he was adept at helping others to heal he privately struggled right to the end of his life with his own loneliness, depression and grief.

Retreat offers us the space to observe our life throughout all its ups and downs. Inevitably we learn that everything that gives us pleasure will also bring pain - and then the very knowledge that life is uncertain, that things are not always going to be wonderful, can bring a sense of acceptance. We can either accept our difficulties as opportunities or become embittered and thus prolong our own suffering. This is a choice that involves a good deal of attention and objectivity on our part. Not easy for sure!

Such a space may help us to understand both the cause and the purpose of our suffering - for unless we do we shall continue to draw to ourselves more of the same. We may see that many of our circumstances are created, moment to moment, from our own attitudes. Every problem then becomes a challenge to accept and transform and every challenge met renews our confidence and enthusiasm for life. By acknowledging our human vulnerability we demonstrate the power of the human spirit to overcome challenges - and to find meaning and purpose in them.

Although suffering doesn't necessarily guarantee spiritual advancement there can sometimes be solace in the knowledge that our difficulties are necessary 'tests' that bring rewards of their own. This may sound like a platitude but it really can never be overstated: *tests help us to grow in stature and show us that we are much bigger than our difficulties*. They help us to get to grips with the mind and its fear of change, loss and above all, death.

We learn that **things** don't last; good times, bad times, all passes by, and everything moves in cycles. We try especially to ignore the uncertainty of our own lifespan; we avoid death for as long as we can. Yet death is an everyday reality- we die every day. Something dies, something is reborn – our cells, our relationships, even our ideas about things. But when we become rooted in our inner life, our death becomes less of a problem. We understand that it is only the smaller part of us that dies, together with our temporary identity, the personality. What remains throughout is our consciousness, the Eternal Thread of Life or Soul. This is beyond suffering.

Creativity and Transformation
Creative pursuits can bring solace in times of stress. They help us to find meaning, to transform suffering into a thing of beauty – a fine painting, a piece of literature, a symphony, a garden, and so on. Artists are transformers. They do more than reflect or interpret life; they turn their life experience into something greater, not by prettying it up but by creating something new and meaningful. That should be the purpose of all inspirational work. Not that we should ignore the darkness at all - it's too important for that - but should instead raise it up, transform it.

Creativity is an essential part of this retreat. It is a natural expression of the soul and can be anything from decorating a room to writing a memoir.

There has never been another 'you' or another 'me' and there never will be. Whatever we create is an expression of that uniqueness. To quote the American writer William Faulkner we create *out of the materials of the human spirit something which did not exist before*.

So, it is vital that we be ourselves – and not what someone else would like us to be! This is our spiritual destiny. We are each born to create and our creations, however humble, live on in the world long after we have said our goodbyes.

Compassion
Suffering can also increase our compassion, that ability to 'feel with' and care better for others. Indeed, it can spur us to alleviate their suffering, as well as our own, in very practical and creative ways.

It's very important that we treat *ourselves* with compassion, especially when we feel lost, devoid of comfort, of answers. This is the Wilderness experience and is a necessary part of our spiritual journey. Remember that while distress is very real for the 'little self' in the world, for the Undying Self it is all part of a much bigger story. The Wilderness eventually leads us beyond our distress and upwards to the Mountain of Revelation itself.

---

[1] *The Relaxation Response* (Dr Herbert Benson and Miriam Z. Clipper) Harper Collins 2009

[2] *Dying to be Me: My Journey from Cancer, to Near Death, to True Healing* (Anita Moorjani) Hay House 2012

[3] The High Place is actually an energy centre, a point between your eyebrows. It is known as the *Ajna* or brow centre, one of seven major centres in the body. In the chapters that follow and the exercises contained in them, we shall constantly return to this High Place, our portable sanctuary.

[4] *A Treatise on White Magic p.53* (Alice A. Bailey) Lucis Publishing Company

Chapter 2
The Wilderness Experience

Somewhere between Heaven and Earth is a State called Perfect Peace (from Return to the Mountain)

Awakening: The Journey to the Mountain

*T*ake *Me to the Mountain!* The words were my own yet I had no idea where they came from. It was Valentine's Day many years ago; my partner had just left me and over a hundred miles away my mother was dying. I reached for a cigarette but the packet was empty; the final straw.

I was taken by surprise, like a small child whose wailing has been silenced by some unexpected distraction. The words interrupted my misery and I now found myself in a high place, somewhat removed from the world.

An unusual peace came upon me and, from that higher perspective I looked down at the unhappy little person, kneeling on the floor below me. For a moment or two it seemed that, despite everything, I was quite untouched by my circumstances. *Everything really is fine up here! I thought. This is just one tiny episode in a Life that has many yesterdays and many tomorrows ...*

Although this small episode didn't forestall the pain of lessons to come it did help me to see that, throughout all our pleasures and pains, life runs in cycles, and that eventually all things pass. It gave me a new perspective - that, as I now realise, of my Undying Self. It was also the beginning of an awareness that every difficult situation may be a preparation for some future work.

Although fleeting, this experience remained with me and *Take Me to the Mountain* became my mantra in times of trouble.

Saying Goodbye

My friendship with Bob lasted seven years. We spent many hours together in his flat, a place of great peace and spiritual nourishment, where no matter how much pain he was in he always made his visitors welcome. He was an excellent cook and took pride in his surroundings. Whenever we said goodbye he would watch me from his window, all the way home or as far as he could still see me. And on days when we didn't meet we spent further hours on the phone. At one point he began to empty his flat of some of its contents – his collection of statues, including an exquisite Green Tara, came to me along with a number of esoteric books. He believed his own death was imminent and began to prepare for it in his own way. And, selfishly, I prepared for it too by avoiding him for a time, protecting myself from the pain of losing him. A further year passed however and it seemed that he may have been wrong.

It was late spring and I had not seen Bob for some days although we had spoken briefly the evening before. He had taken up painting and in a matter of weeks had completed a collection of canvasses. I was looking forward to seeing his latest work. Today for some reason I sensed that something was wrong so I decided to phone. That he did not answer was not unusual really for he would often sleep during the day, especially if he had taken extra painkillers. However, I took his key from the drawer and walked the short distance to his flat where I saw his little blue van parked outside. So, he was home then.

I arrived just as another tenant unlocked the main door so had no need to ring the bell. I climbed the staircase to the first floor where Bob had arranged a miniature garden outside his door – a collection of potted palms and flowers and a large seated Buddha. Unable to get any response when I rang the doorbell, I peered through the letter box. Candles were burning in the hallway and from his room came the familiar scent of incense, Nag Champa, and the sound of Van Morrison playing his favourite track. I took a breath, put my key in the lock and let myself in; it was the first time I had used that key and I felt like an intruder. It took me what seemed like minutes to walk the length of the little hallway. His bedroom door was open. I wondered if he might be sleeping and crept forward, afraid that I might disturb his rest, or worse still scare him to death. The room was dimly lit and the bed angled such that that I could only discern the back of his head and one arm, purple now, that had dropped to his side.

It was an intimate moment – no tears, just a pause and a murmur (*Oh, Bob* ...) - as I reached for my mobile phone.
I had anticipated this time for more than a year, even imagined letting myself in to his flat with the key he had given me for that purpose, for we both knew that when the time came, I would be the one to find him.
I remembered the evening he told me he was dying and my own panic at the thought of life without him. I'd sat then, studying the familiar figure – bald, overweight and virtually toothless - and had a powerful urge to embrace him. I can't ever let you go, I told myself. But in the months that followed my visits grew less frequent, something I have regretted ever since.

How quickly we learn the protocol of death, notifying those who need to know - police, ambulance service, and of course friends and relatives; many we may never have met. Within days I had agreed to help organise and eventually officiate at his funeral, knowing that this was what he would have wished. And when finally it was all over I felt elated rather than tired, fuelled by the extra adrenaline that had kept me in a constant state of alert. I had, I believed, done all my grieving in advance. I felt calm and peaceful, knowing that I had done my best; yet at the same time I was keeping quite busy, hoping somehow to continue not just my own work but his too. I wanted him to be proud of me!

Friends, I knew, were concerned about me. Where were the tears, where the signs of loss? I had rationalized his passing, happy that at last he had found freedom from pain and from the profound sense of loneliness that had dogged him all of his life. Then one day something changed.

Entering the Wilderness
Bob had been visiting my dreams for some time. I think his approach in dream time was a gentle transition; it prepared me for more direct communication later. It is said that our grieving or disbelief in the after-life can make it much harder for our loved ones to contact us but dreams are a useful gateway for them to enter and communicate with us because our conscious mind doesn't interfere. In the first he appeared in a hospital bed, looking a little sad and disorientated. I stroked his arm and remarked on how smooth and real and solid it felt, even though I was aware I was dreaming and that he had passed on. It is commonly believed that those who have been ill for some time often need nursing care on the astral planes before they are ready to continue on their journey. It appeared that Bob was now getting the care, attention and rest that he had needed so badly.

In a later dream he was standing outside a church. I was excited to see him but knew instinctively that our time together was limited. I had so many questions to ask him about the afterlife and what it was like 'over there.' I began by enquiring about his work. No words were spoken however and our conversation was completely telepathic, mind to mind. He pointed to the church and explained wordlessly that he was some kind of guardian and was responsible for all the work that went on within it. I had the sense that he was involved with both the energy of the 'building' itself and the teachings within it. This was ironic since Bob had once visited a local church as a young child, curious to know what went on there. He had been raised in poverty, one of a large family, and often had no shoes on his feet so he must have looked quite a grubby little urchin, standing quietly at the back of the church. As he walked up the aisle to take his place in one of the pews, the horrified priest, expecting trouble, ordered him to leave. Bob never forgot that rejection and the many others that followed throughout his life and that all added to his sense of isolation.

He then began to approach me more directly, sometimes entering that place between sleep and waking too, carried in on a gust of air. I would be awake but quite relaxed and unafraid and suddenly feel his face next to mine, perfectly smooth because of *alopecia universalis*, a condition that had left him devoid of hair. (He'd often liked to tease me, and laughing at my mock prudishness would promise to climb into my bed once he'd 'gone.' But my response was always the same: *Don't you dare!*)

His presence at these times was as real as it ever had been, perhaps more real in a way for he felt even closer. Although I was comforted by our contact sadly it was always too brief. It seemed he now had so much work to do on the other side of the veil that our time together had to be short-lived.

I began to take night time walks, ending up at the block of flats where he'd lived. I'd peer through the glass door to the entrance hall, where for years I'd run up the stairs to meet him. Sometimes I'd place a finger on the doorbell, remembering how I used to wait for the buzz that released the door and allowed me in. (Even now, six years on, I cannot pass the end of that road without mentally saluting him or whispering his name). But back then the memory of him suddenly became too much to bear and when grief could no longer be contained, I entered the Wilderness.

The Wilderness experience can be anything from a broken love affair to losing one's job. It can be triggered by bereavement, an illness, a financial crisis. Confusion, overwhelm, desolation and loss of life's meaning are all feelings associated with the 'wilderness.' In my own case I knew I badly needed some time to myself but had no real means of escape – family responsibilities and a lack of money meant that I had to stay where I was. So how could I find what I needed, where would I find solace, a state of perfect peace? Then I remembered *Return to the Mountain*, the story I had written (and one that Bob had particularly liked), and the answer came clearly: *I would take myself to the Mountain!*

Pulling Back
The 'mountain,' as I had already discovered, is our personal sanctuary, a place of rest. Bob often complained that I never took enough rest. 'Rest while you work,' he would say over and over. 'And rest while you rest!' I began to understand just what this meant now. Once you are relaxed, it actually makes no difference whether you are working or not. You begin to grasp that it's all 'your time' anyway. However, I decided on this occasion to take some time away from work and began to plan a little retreat package for myself. I knew that if I didn't 'book it in advance' it just wouldn't happen. It might work for a day, maybe two, and then life would go back to normal. As you will see, I was not naturally a well disciplined person!

I then remembered the old maxim 'a change is as good as a rest' and had once read in the Agni Yoga teachings[1] that when we are tired, we don't need to stop everything. It is often enough just to do something different instead.
Retreat means to pull back. So, I let people know that for a few days I would be 'pulling back.' Since I wanted this to be *a retreat whilst living in the world*, I explained that I would still be available, if needed, for a short time each evening. I

am accustomed to receiving a good deal of calls but to my surprise the phone rang very little during that time – and what a difference that made!

My domestic routines continued as normal – structure and rhythm are particularly useful for anyone suffering from anxiety and depression, or going through an unhappy change of circumstances. Some kind of daily structure can allow you to feel 'held' and secure. A regular routine that is flexible and not too rigid helps to re-build self-confidence and can alleviate the sense of 'falling apart.'

Revisiting the Mountain

My days always began with a period of 'silent sitting.' Here I took myself to the 'Mountain' and gently brought my attention to my 'high place,' the centre between the eyebrows. This silent time allowed me to fully experience the pain of loss and the shock of my friend's death. Looking out from my high place I found I could both feel and observe it at the same time. It was a time of real letting go. I even began to be a patient and kindly companion to myself instead of the stern task master I had been in the past.

I noticed, really noticed, what I was thinking and how I was feeling. I noticed without trying to change those thoughts or feelings.

I began to notice so much more too – that I was breathing (rather badly!) for instance. When we feel pain we tend to hold our breath. Shallow breathing is a defence and numbs our feelings for a while but it also keeps them locked in. Noticing that you are breathing is incredibly powerful. Somehow a breath, consciously breathed, makes the whole body relax. A few conscious breaths calm the mind too and restore energy if you are tired.

I noticed other little things that would normally pass me by - routine activities like washing the dishes or feeding the cat.

By 'noticing' what I was doing I was able to relax more. I planned simple but nutritious meals, taking more time to prepare and enjoy them. I bought enough food in advance to last me for the first week – plenty of fresh fruit and vegetables, and grains such as quinoa or rice.

Re-creation and Having Fun
Since I had no means of escaping to some far off paradise, I did prioritise time for daily walks. Contact with nature, whether in the back garden, a local park or nearest open countryside, is an absolute essential for any retreat.

Exercise helps to keep the energies flowing. Unfortunately I cannot swim but I do love to walk. Brisk walking can quickly transform emotions such as sadness or anger.

Routine and discipline were stabilizing factors for me during this time; silent sitting, creativity, nourishment and exercise all had their place in each day. But so did spontaneity and having fun – whatever happened to take my fancy. I found time for recreation. Sometimes this would mean reading something by a favourite author at bedtime or dancing to rock music with the blinds closed!

What an interesting word that is: *re-creation!* Creative projects were a vital part of my retreat and for me this meant drawing and painting. Any creative activity, such as decorating, making music, writing, gardening or cooking will work equally well. There are so many ways to be creative (see Chapter 3).

Creativity can be a meditation in itself. Whenever we are absorbed in some purposeful task we are focused and one-pointed and this is very much like the meditative state. In times of quiet reflection or contemplative action we are also very open to receive impressions from our soul.

My awareness became sharper - everything I did was 'noticed,' from eating my breakfast to emptying the rubbish bin. I noticed my Inner Voice so much more and increasingly it became my guide. Suddenly it seemed that my 'everyday retreat' was now also a period of training.

Five Pathways to Immortality

It was during my morning silent sittings that I began to receive regular guidance in the form of a dictated message on a particular theme. These 'messages' continued for some time and eventually became twice weekly rather than daily. They were also accompanied by a series of paintings to illustrate them).

Months later I looked at the messages again and found that some – just forty of them - could be shared. I gathered these together and noticed that they fell neatly into five groups: **Silence, Self-Knowing, Discipleship, Service and Love, all Pathways to Immortality**. Then within each group were eight messages, enough for forty cards and perfect material for a guided retreat!

My first public retreat (*Take Me to the Mountain*) took place in an old, rather quirky country house over a long weekend, Friday evening to Sunday afternoon. (All the retreats to date have been non-residential, mainly to emphasise the value of 'living and working in the world'). At the start of each session I would place a guidance card on each chair and ask participants to contemplate its meaning. The result was extraordinary, and as surprising to me as to them. The significance of the messages became unfailingly pertinent and poignant and I cannot remember how many boxes of cards I sold on that first retreat weekend.

Even while I am writing this book, I am still working my way through the messages. I've lost count of how many times I've done this but each time I discover something new. Although the pack can be used in the usual way, a card selected at random whenever the need is felt, I do recommend using them in sequence for the 40 day retreat.

There is something mysterious and meaningful about this period of time and with each cycle of use comes a deepening of understanding and a lightening of spirit.

I have also used the cards in my healing practice to great effect, and with surprising success in telephone consultations. I have been asked repeatedly to share them further afield and to make this simple everyday retreat available to a wider audience. It is my great pleasure then to invite you to come with me to the Mountain, and to make retreat a way of life, wherever you happen to be and whatever you are doing.

What follows is a guide, not a rule book, and you are encouraged to adapt the simple exercises to meet your own needs - and even to devise your own.

NB. I recommend that you read this book in its entirety before embarking on retreat. This way you will familiarise yourself in advance with the daily practices and will already have developed an attitude of retreat.

---

[1] The Agni Yoga Society was founded in 1920 by Nicholas Roerich and his wife Helena. The philosophy that gives it its name is contained in a series of books published by the Society.

Chapter 3
Planning your 40-day & 40-night Retreat

Being on retreat while living in the world is very simple indeed but you will need to plan ahead just as though you were going away. Although this is a guidebook I have no intention of giving you a long list of things to accomplish – you probably have more than enough to do already! Its purpose is to make your life easier by using your usual everyday activities as material for retreat - a retreat where you are living (and working) in the world. Each day begins with a period of silent sitting and ends with an Evening Review that will benefit you while you sleep.

NB. If it is not practical for you to do the full 40 days and 40 nights in one go you may like to try an 8 day mini-retreat instead, beginning with the Pathway of Silence. The other Pathways will then form the basis of future retreats whenever you choose.
It is strongly recommended that you repeat your retreat at frequent intervals.

There is no need for anyone else to know you are on retreat – apart from those you live with of course. Your daily routine will be exactly the same apart from 30 minutes in the morning and evening when you will be unavailable. These will be your 'silent sitting' times so you may need to negotiate with those involved. You may wish to limit phone calls and internet use (strongly advised at this time), but otherwise your retreat will go unnoticed – from the outside at least. The idea is for you to develop an 'attitude of retreat,' one that will serve you for the rest of your life. Above all, my wish is that you will enjoy it.

For many people with family and work commitments, 'spare' time is a luxury. Yet however little you may have it is *how* you spend that time that counts.

I am always trying to squeeze more time out of my day and frequently find myself running late, or arriving just on time, by the skin of my teeth! I used to stay up far too late at night, believing that I would gain more personal time – quiet time, in fact, undisturbed by phone calls or visitors.

Restfulness: it's all my time anyway!

The secret is to remember that ''all time is our own,' no matter what the demands. Think how it is when you embark on some task with resentment. You wish you were elsewhere, doing something else. You want time to pass quickly. Next time you are frustrated or bored to tears try saying: 'But this is actually still my time,' and it will change how you feel – about your work, household chores, and even having to spend time with people you'd rather avoid. It's all your own time! I feel I can't emphasize this enough; it is fundamental to our everyday retreat and just makes life so much easier. Remind yourself often and you will no longer feel as annoyed and deprived – and you might even enjoy it.

So, relax while you're working and relax while you're resting. It's all the same. Of course it takes practice to develop restfulness but it is all part of developing an attitude of retreat whilst living in the world.

Noticing

'Noticing' is another vital attitude of retreat. When we relax we are more likely to pay attention to the life within and around us – our breathing, our body, our thoughts and feelings as well as our actions. Observation leads to detachment, a practice that helps us to deal with the ups and downs of life and not be overwhelmed by them; a way of mastering our wayward emotions without suppressing them. And practice is the answer: practise with the little things, everyday situations and encounters, until observation or detachment becomes second-nature.

To watch our life from a little distance is to see ourselves more clearly. We suddenly recognise certain habitual thoughts, fears that obstruct our peace of mind. We also spot little personality mannerisms and how we say and do things to achieve certain ends. Likewise when we give our full attention to the moment and whatever we happen to be doing, we become more relaxed.

We start to notice the great gap between our outer life (where nothing lasts forever), and the Inner Life which is constant and eternal and sense a happiness that can only exist from within, in the eternal realm of the soul. Retreat reinforces our sense of living 'inside out.'

Routine

Each day on retreat has its own suggested routine and begins with your **30 minute Morning Practice**. (This will be explained in detail in the next chapter). It's a matter of personal preference whether you bathe or shower before or after your morning practice but I suggest you have a flask of hot water or herbal tea to hand for that added comfort and to help you to wake up. You will also need your set of **Take Me to the Mountain** Guidance Cards if you possess any (if not, the messages are included here anyway), plus a notebook or journal.

- If you share a bedroom you may need to use somewhere else for your Morning and Evening Practice. Ideally it begins as soon as you wake up – and before you get out of bed – with a period of **gentle, conscious breathing (5 minutes).**

- **Next you will think of the Mountain, solid, ancient, and unmoved by wind or storm (5 minutes)**. As described in Chapter 1, you imagine your feet as its base, anchored deeply in the earth. This is a wonderfully grounding exercise and can be practised at any time of day or night, especially if you are feeling anxious.

- **You will then be ready to go to your High Place, the mountain top (5 minutes)**. This, as you already know, is actually an energy centre between the eyebrows: the *Ajna* centre, a place where you rest and steadily observe yourself.

- **Now follows your Message for the day (5 minutes)**. Even if you do nothing else on this retreat the daily Message is essential reading and will set the tone of the day. As outlined in Chapter 1, each message belongs to one of five *Pathways to Immortality* (Silence, Self-Knowing, Discipleship, Service and Love). This message will help you to make your **Morning Resolve**, an intention we set for the day **(5 minutes)**.

- Finally, you can use your remaining time to record any insights in your notebook or journal, or continue with your 'silent sitting' **(10 minutes)**.

Daily Activities

The rest of your day until the **Evening Review** will be spent relaxing, even – and especially! - if you are at work! Apart from a lunch break, do try to have a short morning and afternoon break (even 5 minutes is enough) for silent sitting and conscious breathing; a time to rest in your High Place.

- Choose any daily activity, for example preparing or

eating a meal. While you prepare and eat your food, **relax**. Whenever you are washing the dishes, notice you are washing the dishes, and rest - without wishing you could be doing something else! This applies to any activity, of course. When you are travelling, stuck in a traffic jam, enjoy the journey - use this time for retreat. It certainly takes less energy.

- Watch your thoughts from time to time and notice how you respond to others.

- When you speak, be mindful of the tone of your voice and the effect your words will have. Notice the energy they carry.

- Notice the effect others have on *you*. See what raises or lowers your mood: conversations, T.V. programmes, and so on. We can liken our 'inner life' to a fire that needs our attention in order to keep it burning brightly. Recognise what feeds and what dims your inner light.

- Notice how you speak to yourself; encourage rather than criticise yourself; be a wise and loving guide, not a stern task master.

- Listen to others with full, un-distracted attention.

- BE YOURSELF and notice when you are not being quite true to yourself!

- Pay great attention to each passing moment, so that there are no longer either 'ordinary' or 'extraordinary' moments; there is only NOW. When you do this every moment counts, every moment is special.

- **And finally, enjoy this time!**

Evening Practice
In the Tibetan Buddhist tradition there is a certain preparation for death called the *Life Review*. This is intended to help the dying person to make their journey, free of any unresolved thoughts and feelings. It is a time to face one's self honestly and sincerely and to make peace.
The Evening Review is a great opportunity to clear the mind and make peace before the journey into sleep.

NB. This winding-down period will also include time for your journal and reading (anything conducive to sleep and not over-stimulating).

Self-Care
Your retreat is an opportunity to take extra care of yourself.
Let's take nutrition first. There is no universally perfect diet so what I suggest is one that is suited to your own needs.
Simple, nutritious food will give your digestion and immune system a boost. I recommend fresh, organic, whole-food, preferably vegetarian, although fish may occasionally be included. Eat plenty of fresh fruit, salads and vegetables, whole grains and pulses. Avoid processed foods and refined sugar. Homemade soups are excellent and particularly easy to prepare. Above all your food and its preparation should be enjoyable!

Have access to filtered water, the purest you can find. You will need to drink at least 7-8 glasses of water (hot or cold) each day. Herbal or fruit teas are excellent as well as white or green teas. Coffee is best avoided (although substitutes made with chicory or barley can be used).

Exercise (30 minutes, split into two parts if necessary) at least 3 times a week. Movement increases our physical, mental and emotional circulation. It raises the spirits and releases tension caused by worry, anger, irritation, grief and so on. Walking is especially good as it can stimulate creative thought. It also allows for time spent in Nature. A few minutes spent each day, 'touching the earth,' is deeply healing. Time spent in the garden, a local park or countryside, surrounded by the wonders of creation, deepens our appreciation and sense of belonging to the world we live in.

Choose an activity that you actually enjoy: walking, swimming, dancing, yoga or Tai Chi, etc. are all great forms of exercise.

Creativity (whenever possible)

There are many ways to be creative. You don't have to be a skilled artist, musician or writer either: you can express your inner life (soul) through the most elementary and simple drawings – doodles - or create beautiful mandalas. Or you may choose to work on a larger scale, using wide brush strokes and whole body movements.

Alternatively you might decide to transform your environment by decorating a room or planting flowers in the garden – whatever you enjoy, do it; that is the main thing.

If you are musical you may find that beautiful harmonies come to you, or unexpected words in the form of stories, poems, letters or even guidance of some kind. Just relax and allow the inspiration to come. You may think of questions you need answers to; again, relax and write whatever comes into your waiting mind.

Creative self-expression is excellent therapy at any time and helps us to get some perspective on our life. Through the act of writing especially we get to see ourselves at a distance; and when we see our life on the page we also gain understanding – of the choices we have made and what we have learned from them. Writing also stimulates the memory.

Planning ahead

Before you begin your retreat, whether it is for 8 days or 40, I suggest that you allow at least 2 days preparation. Treat this as a very practical time just as you would if you were making a journey. Here then is a check list to get you started:

1. **Plan your shopping** for simple, fresh and nutritious food for the first week (See Self Care).

2. **Remember that retreat means to 'draw back.'** Alert others to the fact that you will be on retreat and explain what this means. Place a limit on phone calls and e-mails, one that is practical and helpful for you. Create a list of guidelines for yourself and others.

3. **Begin to develop an 'attitude of retreat' in advance:** *Breathe* and know you are breathing. *Rest* while you are working and *rest while you are resting.* (This means you will notice whenever you get stressed – and why). Remember that it's all your time anyway, regardless of what you are doing! Enjoy each moment and *Smile!*

4. **NOTICE!** Leave yourself little reminders to 'notice' – 'Post-It' notes on the bathroom mirror, in the kitchen, on your bedside table, in the car, reminding you to 'notice' or 'rest.' Rest in your 'High Place' and you'll be more aware of everything you are thinking, saying and doing. This will also increase your intuition or 'inner knowing.'

5. **Be flexible and resourceful**. If quiet time is not feasible at home because of young children or other dependents, plan your silent sitting for a more suitable time of day. For instance you might use your lunch break at work or even sit in your car for those silent moments.

6. **Invest in good ear plugs** for your 'silent sittings' if noise is a problem. (I find silicone earplugs the most

effective).

7. **Plan your daily agenda in advance**. Each day will have a similar routine but the timings will be your own. Details follow in Chapter 4 and include your **Morning 'Silent Sitting,' Message from the Mountain, Morning Resolve, Journal keeping** (morning or evening); and an **Evening Review** before sleep. You can timetable other activities to suit your own agenda, including **exercise** and **creative activities** of your own choice. Be flexible and always adapt your retreat to suit your circumstances.
8. **Have ready some essential oils** for bathing or a lotion for self-massage after bathing or showering. I find lavender, frankincense and rose especially good but you may have your own special favourites.

9. **Before bed, prepare a flask of hot water for your waking drink**. Add a slice of lemon, lime or some herbal/fruit/white/green tea if preferred.

10. **Have your *Take Me to the Mountain* Guidance Cards ready** (or alternatively use the Messages in the book). I advise using the cards in order and when you come to the end, begin again … and again. I can guarantee that they will offer up new meaning for you each time.

11. **Keep a journal or notebook** to hand for your morning and evening 'silent sitting' times.

12. **Plan to go to bed a little earlier than usual**, and allow more time at the start of the day. (Anyone who knows me well will probably be raising an eyebrow now as they know that early nights have not always come naturally to me. There is no doubt however that early nights and early rising have definite health benefits).[1]

13. **Treat this time as a holiday**, a real opportunity for rest. It is to be enjoyed so why not make the most of it!

---

[1] According to many ancient traditions, the life span of the human body is 120 years. To achieve this it is deemed important to live in harmony with the natural rhythms of your body, the soul's vehicle of expression. When your body is healthy, your soul is able to fulfill its highest potential.

Part 2
On Retreat

Chapter 4
Arriving: The Pathway of Silence

There are many pathways to the Mountain and one of these is the Pathway of Silence.
Walk with me a while but slowly for we are in no hurry.
Silence makes us aware of this moment, a precious unending moment. It makes us remember Life, our precious unending Life. So, let us enjoy this moment together!

Silence is the essential starting point from which all other Pathways proceed. It is through Silence that you reach your High Place, the Mountain Top. Each moment spent in Silence creates a greater connection with your Soul or Undying Self. How then can you strengthen that connection? Here follows your first 8 day 'silent' retreat ...

Day 1 (This will serve as a model for each of the 40 days; only your Message from the Mountain, Morning Resolve and Evening Review will change in content)

1. Morning Practice:

Your Breathing Space (5 minutes)
Welcome - you are now on retreat! Retreat offers us a breathing space, literally. It's also a time for inspiration; that's what the word inspire means: to *breathe in*.

As soon as you open your eyes begin to notice that you are breathing. Breathe … enjoy breathing in … and breathing out. How easy, how beautiful a breath is, a symbol of life's

renewal. Enjoy each Breath of Life. And as you breathe, really *know* that you are breathing. Hold breath in your body for an instant before releasing it. Now enjoy the sensation of letting it go. For a moment or two, let breathing be the most important thing in your life, the only thing.
As you continue to breathe - knowing that you are breathing - your mind will soon become very quiet and still.

In these first few moments of retreat your body will instinctively fall into a state of rest; your mind will grow quiet but alert. Let yourself wake up fully and then have a gentle stretch before sitting up.

Sitting upright, sip a glass or cup of hot water, etc. from your flask and continue to breathe gently. Notice how your body is feeling. Appreciate your body, your home for this lifetime; enjoy the feeling of the earth beneath you.
Notice any sounds of life around you without being disturbed by them. Notice the inner sounds too – your thoughts - without being interested or disturbed by them. Maybe you are not very used to silent sitting or even sitting still. Even though you may be doing nothing your mind can still be active; day-dreaming, planning, remembering. So notice how quiet it becomes when you are no longer interested in your thoughts. You know that thoughts are coming and going but you are not giving them any attention.

Experience yourself as the observer of your breathing; of your body; of your thoughts.
Feel yourself, alert and alive in this present moment – NOW!
You have now entered the *Pathway of Silence.*

Become the Mountain (5 minutes)
Try picturing a mountain: solid, ageless and anchored in the earth; unmoved by winds and storms. Now imagine your feet as the base of your mountain, also rooted in the earth. You should now begin to feel some of that solidity,

agelessness and poise in your own body. You are now so solid that no external force can shake you, nothing – not even your own thoughts. This is a powerfully grounding exercise, especially when you are feeling threatened or anxious. Use it at any time during the day. For now continue to breathe gently.

Go to your High Place (5 minutes)
Take Me to the Mountain: these words have the effect of taking you directly to your High Place (that place between your eyebrows) where you will be poised and ready to face the new day. Repeat them silently and use them as an invocation throughout the day, whenever you feel the need. Without losing your sense of solidity as the mountain, begin to notice your thoughts again, without being disturbed by them. Let thoughts come and go just as your breathing rises and falls. Slowly climb your mountain to reach the peak, (your brow), while still being aware of the earth beneath your feet. Here, in your High Place is your refuge or retreat. Here you can quietly observe your own life and everything going on around you. In fact, whenever you are anxious I suggest you try using *Take Me to the Mountain* as a simple invocation. It takes us to a place of safety, closer to our Deathless state or Soul. This state of observing or 'noticing' is a form of meditation in itself. I like to call it 'silent sitting.'

Message from the Mountain (5 minutes of reading and reflection):

1
Silence

Draw deeply from the Well of Silence.
Now and then throughout the day take a minute's silence in remembrance of your Self. In this silent time you may reflect in gratitude on your life.
You may offer a prayer for blessing, for courage or for healing.
A prayer for others.

And know that your prayer has already been answered, the blessing given. All is well at the Centre.
Losing awareness is moving away from that centre, becoming un-conscious. ***Let there be no beginning, nor end to your consciousness!***
Your Centre is your throne of power,
*Your Centre is who you are, your **Be-ing.***

The Morning Resolve (5 minutes)
This is an intention we set for the day. Let's remember that we make memories for others as well ourselves - so with this first Message we have a perfect theme for our Morning Resolve. We do not know exactly what today will bring but we can set the tone for this day by deciding *how we will be and, therefore, how our day will be, regardless of what it brings.* Another valuable attitude to adopt while on retreat!

The message reminds us to draw deeply from Silence throughout the coming day, whatever we may be doing, and to wonder at the miracle of our own life. We are also invited to offer up a prayer for whatever we most need today; and to offer up a prayer for others too.

It urges us to rest in our Centre. Imagine, seated as kings or queens on our own throne of power! And doesn't it give that same sense of poise and solidity that 'being the mountain does' too?

Closing
Continue to breathe gently and prepare to close your Morning Practice. Remain in your High Place as much as you can throughout your daily activities and with that same sense of Silence, of 'being the mountain,' unmoved by wind or storm. Enjoy your day!

2. Evening Practice (30 minutes or as required): this will be repeated before sleep throughout your retreat

The Evening Review
Make sure you are comfortable and relaxed. Begin by 'breathing and knowing you are breathing.' Go to your High Place and before sleep, look back with gratitude on the day that is ending. Notice your thoughts and actions, your responses to the day's events. Without criticism, regret, blame or congratulations (this is difficult and takes practice!), notice how you have lived.

Notice the little slights that have knocked you off balance. Words that have touched the tender parts of you, rubbed up against old wounds. For the very sensitive, any hostile glance or 'note' of envy, criticism or malice will be registered at once and will disturb the quiet pool of emotion.

Notice too those same 'notes' created by your own mind: envious, critical, irritable thoughts.

Notice the things that have pleased you; the lessons that have been learned and those that need more attention. Then let it all go.

Journal notes and reading (as required)
Note any insights you have received today, particularly any observations connected with your daily Message, Morning Resolve or Evening Review.

At some point you may have some direct inspiration from your soul – a message of your own – that you can record here.

Reading can facilitate restful sleep but make sure it is nothing too stimulating. This is, you will remember, a retreat for both day and night.

When you are ready for sleep, continue to breathe gently. Notice the rise and fall of your breathing until your body rests and your mind becomes quiet. Soon you will notice that space between waking and dreaming and be ready to enter the deep Silence of sleep.

END OF DAY CHECK LIST:

- **BREATHE!**
- **NOTICE!**
- **BE THE MOUNTAIN**
- **REST IN YOUR HIGH PLACE**
- **ENJOY THE SILENCE WITHIN YOU**

Day 2
Morning Practice (as before)

Breathing Space
Keep your eyes closed and begin to notice that you are breathing. Just that: notice. Now notice your body and while you breathe (knowing that you are breathing) let your body rest. Notice how you are feeling this morning, just notice. Next notice the stream of thoughts that flow while you are breathing; and resting; and feeling. Staying very relaxed but fully awake, become aware of 'you,' the one who watches the breathing and the body and the thoughts.

Now, in this state of restful awareness read Message 2 :

2
Peace

Guard your silence and do not complain that another disturbs your peace.
The greater disturbance is of your own making.
Even now as we speak you know the truth of this and delight in it. Remember these words:
Peace is only a thought away
Do not hide your humanity; instead, raise it up!
The sadness you may feel today is tomorrow's joy.
Be peaceful in your sadness and also in your joy.
Today is just a tiny episode in a life that has many yesterdays and many tomorrows. When you enter your place of silence, time stands still and you touch the Peace of Eternity

The Morning Resolve (5 minutes)
The world may not be silent around you but that doesn't matter in the least. The simple practice of silent sitting is all that is needed. Sit then, with your eyes closed, and *notice*.
Silence doesn't mean that the birds have to stop singing or that traffic must come to a standstill. Life goes on beyond our control. It is an inner silence that you find along this Pathway. It is technically possible to meditate with a football match on the television and rock music playing next door. Try it! You can even learn to recognise your inner silence while listening or speaking to someone else. Try that too. When you operate from the silent place within you, you are very 'tuned in,' to Undying Self as well as to others. Peace is instantly there – just a thought away – because you are training your mind to be quiet. And when you are unhappy you can even be peaceful with that feeling too, remembering life's bigger picture. Today is only a very small part of your own Life Story.

In retreat you give space for your Inner Life or Soul and you can with a little imagination, easily create conditions of peace and silence for yourself everyday.
So whatever your Morning Resolve may be, greet today peacefully, positively, and be open to receive whatever you need most at this time.

Closing
As before, continue to breathe and prepare to close your Morning Practice. 'Be the Mountain' and remain in your High Place as often as you can today. May you have a silent and peaceful day!

Evening Practice (as before)

The Evening Review / Journal notes and reading (as before)
How did Peace feature in your experience of today? The

Evening Review is always an opportunity to make peace with yourself and others. Resist the temptation to judge yourself harshly. Instead, have an understanding of your own difficulties. Use compassion, smile at your own efforts – or lack of effort! You will find it easier to understand other people and to imagine the difficulties life throws up for them too. A little compassion for yourself gives you the courage and inspiration to try again another day. Remember that your retreat doesn't end here: may you have a nourishing and peaceful sleep!

END OF DAY CHECK LIST:

- **BREATHE!**
- **NOTICE!**
- **BE THE MOUNTAIN**
- **REST IN YOUR HIGH PLACE**
- **REMEMBER: PEACE IS ONLY A THOUGHT AWAY!**

Day 3
Morning Practice (as before)

3
Recognition

Go down through the layers now,
Layers of emotion built up over your lifetimes and difficult to penetrate;
Layers of illusion built on fear and separation.
Do you long for acknowledgment?
Move, ever onwards and inwards, to that clear light within.
Here, at the still point, there is nothing between you and your own God-Self.
Here there is no vanity; no pride; no anger; no guilt
No separation
Here, at your Centre, you neither set yourself up nor put yourself down.

And if you are still seeking recognition
You have not yet reached your Centre of Silence
For it is at your Centre that you recognise Your Self

The Morning Resolve

When we allow too little time for self-care we can end up feeling resentful, unacknowledged and overlooked. Self-care is not the same as self-absorption. It means taking responsibility for our own well-being without placing demands on others. It also means that we view ourselves from a different perspective; one where we are in perfect balance, neither higher nor lower than anyone else.

True self-worth comes from identifying with our own God Self – the Undying Self - at the Centre of our Life. So, breathe; become the Mountain, rest in your High Place; and give yourself all the attention you need. Resolve to care for yourself in this way throughout the day and you will find you need less acknowledgment and approval from others.

Closing

Breathe gently and prepare to close your morning practice. Marvel at the miracle of your own Life as you care deeply for yourself throughout the day. May your spirits be raised!

Evening Practice (as before)

The Evening Review / Journal notes and reading (as before) Notice whether increased care and attention to yourself has changed your response to others. Take time to ponder on any changes you have made today, however subtle. End the day with a prayer of gratitude for your own Life.

END OF DAY CHECK LIST:

- **BREATHE!**
- **PAY ATTENTION TO YOURSELF!**
- **BE THE MOUNTAIN**
- **REST IN YOUR HIGH PLACE, A PLACE OF PERFECT BALANCE**
- **CARE DEEPLY FOR YOURSELF AT ALL TIMES**

Day 4
Morning Practice

4
Power

Relax that the mind may rest;
And in rest it will open.
Let mind be free to explore the stillness and silence of itself.
See; feel; imagine Light as it enters your mind.
Let Light show you what is real.
See, feel, imagine potential (or power), dormant in your still and silent mind.
See now who or what has dominion over you.
Who or what can, in truth, hold that power?
Let Light show you what is unreal;
Let Light show you your own Power

The Morning Resolve

Retreat is a wonderful opportunity to cast light on the mind. It is a time to examine your thoughts, separate them out, and see where they take you. Perhaps you can learn to be a little more open-minded and see when you are inflexible in your attitudes. (Although we may pride ourselves on our tolerance and understanding, secretly we all have our little prejudices!).

Whenever you go to the Mountain, notice the thoughts that enter your silent sitting. Stand at a little distance. Notice how your mind works. Where does it lead you? Are your thoughts helpful, kindly? Or are they fearful; suspicious; disruptive? How powerful is their effect on your mood today? Again, just notice. Without trying to stop them you can decide if they are going to run your day. Relax! Let your mind rest and give room for your intuition to guide you. Be the Mountain and trust in its power – your own power. Being open-minded involves discernment. Resolve to notice your thoughts today and your own power to discern what is real. See too when your mind is closed, attached to a particular opinion. How much you can discover about yourself today!

Closing
Breathe calmly and prepare to close your morning practice.

The Evening Review / Journal notes and reading
Without wanting to change anything, what have you learned about yourself today? Shine a light on yourself. What have you noticed about the power of your thoughts? Have you been led astray by them or guided by your intuition? How open-minded have you been? As the day draws to a close, let your body and mind rest. Look back with compassion on your human self. Look back with compassion on others.

END OF DAY CHECK LIST:

- **BREATHE!**
- **RELAX – AND LET YOUR MIND OPEN**
- **NOTICE HOW YOUR MIND WORKS**
- **SHINE A LIGHT ON YOURSELF**

Day 5
Morning Practice

5
Rest

Rest often and deeply.
Rest while you rest, as you have often been told.
Emotions rise ... and subside.
Fear neither the silence of night nor your own loneliness.
Those who move away from you keep the way clear
For your continuing journey
Fear not the solitude of death for, in truth, your journey continues!
Are you not one with Us?
How then can you fear isolation or abandonment?
Words are not needed now.
Sit with your eyes closed and receive Our Love for you
Let Love reach your Centre
Let Love be your name

The Morning Resolve
This message reminds us to rest, for even when think we are relaxed, we can always relax a little more! In our silent times uncomfortable memories and emotions can sometimes arise and it is then that we are urged to notice them without trying to change the way we feel. Insecurities such as loneliness and fear of abandonment can surface. *Accept!* People often avoid silence, just as they avoid their own company. They prefer to be active and believe that to be alone is a bad and frightening thing. Having contact with others is wonderful but it has to be balanced with solitude.

As we forge a deeper union with our true Self we cannot help but change. Alongside this the company we choose also changes, just as our interests may. Individuals naturally fall away from our circle. *Let go!* This makes room for others who are more suited to our changing self. Life is full of arrivals and departures but the journey itself continues. When we settle down and rest in our own Centre there is no silence to fear, no discomfort in aloneness. There is only Love. May love be your companion today ...

Closing
Remain strong and poised as the Mountain and gently prepare to close your Morning Practice in an attitude of restfulness.

The Evening Review / Journal notes and reading
How has your 'attitude of rest' transformed your day? Relax now as you reflect on the past few hours. Again, look back on 'how you have been' with infinite patience and understanding but also honesty. Let nothing escape your attention. Have there been opportunities to accept; to let go; to love?

When you feel fully reconciled and at peace with yourself and with the day, prepare to receive the Blessing of Love offered to you in the morning's Message. Let Love reach your Centre. Let Love be your name.

Let go and enjoy the deep rest of sleep ahead of you.

END OF DAY CHECK LIST:

- **REST!**
- **LET GO**
- **RECEIVE**
- **LOVE**

Day 6
Morning Practice

6
Be-ing

We observe with joy the love that streams forth from your Centre;
Of this you must remain conscious in each waking moment
And also in your sleep
Let that same love stream also within and beyond you,
That all touched by your love
(Whether this be your own cells or the stranger in the shop)
Be filled with the joy of Be-ing.
The joy you feel now is nothing to that which awaits you!

The Morning Resolve

This Message follows perfectly the one before it. It is time to be aware of your true nature, Undying Love. Every moment is an opportunity to love. Love is effortless, it simply requires a willingness to be open and experience something that is already there, in your heart. Each time you breathe, see; feel; imagine love circulating within you. There is nothing you need do: just let it flow. This simple exercise is remarkably powerful. Imagining the current of love moving through your body is deeply healing. Bathe in it for a while. Resolve to radiate this love to everyone who comes close to you today – in fact, to anyone you happen to think of. As in prayer, there are no boundaries of time or space to prevent the flow of love. A thought of love will always reach its target and be felt, even subconsciously.

NOTICE the you who lives right at the centre; the one who always was and always will be - the one who loves without limits.

When we allow too little time for this 'Self at our Centre' we can end up feeling unsatisfied, off-centre and maybe unloved. True self-worth comes from identifying with this Love at the Centre of our Life. **Indeed, Love is at the centre of all Life**. It does not discriminate or find one more worthy of love than another. You and I are loved unreservedly no matter what we have done or how little we think we deserve it. Love is what you and I are made of. So, breathe; and allow yourself all the love and attention you need.

Closing

Breathe gently and prepare to close your meditation. Marvel at the miracle of your own Life as you care deeply for yourself throughout the day.

Continue to enjoy this circulation of love within you and remember that it will radiate from you without any conscious effort. Every glance, every word, every touch from you is a vehicle of love. Love will lift the spirits like nothing else. May you have a joyful day!

The Evening Review / Journal notes and reading

Notice whenever there have been opportunities to practise and receive love. Now see if there has been any resistance to love. Remember always to reflect on the day with honesty and detachment – and a good deal of patience and understanding. There is never cause to feel daunted. Where there have been opportunities missed, resolve to see things differently tomorrow.

Finish your Evening Review with the Morning Review exercise: each time you breathe, see; feel; imagine love circulating within you. Know that you are loved now and into eternity. Let love be your final thought as you prepare for sleep.

END OF DAY CHECK LIST:

- **THINK LOVE**
- **BREATHE LOVE**
- **BATHE IN LOVE**
- **RADIATE LOVE**

Day 7
Morning Practice

7
Contemplation

You see the consequences of moving away from your Centre,
The consequences of fear?
Your mind - caught up in conflict - creates confusion and yet more fear.
Your mind, responding to fear, makes unwise choices
Which take you still further from your Centre.
The real you never leaves your Centre of Silence.
The real you is in an eternal state of contemplation.
Always continue your silent sitting even after you have opened your eyes.
Recall this time whenever you gaze upon another living being.
Bless others with your silence;
The deep well of silence that lies beneath your words.

The Morning Resolve

We are almost at the end of the first Pathway to the Mountain. Today we have a reminder to remain within our Centre of Silence. How easily we become caught up in the world! And how quickly we react to circumstances! The mind becomes distorted by fear and creates yet more fear, more difficulties.

Fear is never far from our thoughts but worrying alone will achieve nothing. Remember to 'be the Mountain' whenever you feel anxious and out of control. Then go to your High Place. Here you can contemplate wise, well-considered choices, based on a desire for the highest good. Your intuition is more finely tuned when you are calm. That is why Silence is vital to your well-being; a silence that exists behind everything you think and do.

Pay great attention to each passing moment, so that there are no longer just 'ordinary' moments or 'special' moments or 'difficult' moments; there is only NOW. When you do this every moment counts, every moment is sacred.

Closing
Contemplate. Bless yourself with Silence; bless others with Silence. Let Silence be the backdrop to your day.

The Evening Review / Journal notes and reading
How has fear affected you today? How have you responded to fearful thoughts and imaginings? How do you usually respond in a crisis?

Be very compassionate and understanding with your fearful little self. To get some sense of perspective remember that this is just one day in a long life of yesterdays and tomorrows. See how each moment has counted, each moment is sacred.

May you now enter the Deep Silence of Sleep.

END OF DAY CHECK LIST:

- **BE THE MOUNTAIN**
- **REST IN YOUR HIGH PLACE**
- **ENTER THE DEEP WELL OF SILENCE**
- **BLESS OTHERS WITH YOUR SILENCE**
- **LET EACH MOMENT COUNT**

Day 8
Morning Practice

8
Intuition

We have to prepare you physically to withstand increased pressure
Materially and on the Inner Planes.
You are still too quick to react, with annoyance when things go wrong
Or when others let you down.
Let go.
Attend to what you can and let that be enough.
Cultivate impersonality.
You must be unshakeable by outside forces –
Imperfections, irritations, criticism and the like.
Choose wisely your daily activities,
Spending no more time on your affairs than you need,
Especially when you become tired.
Allow these quiet times to be sacred, undisturbed by other demands.
Your appointment with your Self is vital.
It will help to maintain and improve your energy levels
And guide your whole system towards harmony.
It will also increase your intuition.
This, you are beginning to notice, is becoming more finely tuned.
This is both your study time and an opportunity for deep rest.
Your capacity to learn is expanding;
You will learn more than you realise.

The Morning Resolve

We have now reached the end of the Pathway of Silence and must prepare for the next stage of our journey, The Pathway of Self-Knowing. This rather long message does just that. It emphasises the need for on-going silence. Your morning and evening appointments are already beginning to make you more aware, more intuitive. These silent sittings will continue to support you as your awareness deepens. This is an exciting message – it hints at further growth and revelations to come.

Of course, each Pathway contains elements of the others: within Silence there are the seeds of Self-Knowing. Here too we find the Master; the Teacher, our Soul. In Silence the quiet mind serves the Soul and learns what it is to Love.

Today discern what is necessary – do only what is needed.
Now more than ever you must be detached. This also means learning to take things less personally, less seriously perhaps. Rest in your High Place and this will become easier. You will soon get a new sense of perspective.
Watch yourself more than ever now: notice what knocks you off balance throughout the day – and be prepared! Embody courage and stability by 'being the Mountain.'
Pause; breathe - whenever you are tempted to react. Then trust your intuition and let it guide you.

Closing
Continue your silent sitting as you prepare to meet the day. Take your quiet time with you wherever you go. Breathe!

The Evening Review / Journal notes and reading
Enjoy this quiet time, the end of your first 8 day retreat. Reflect on the overall experience and what it has given you. Reflect on today as Silence merges with Self-Knowing. What has today revealed to you about yourself? Remember the ancient maxim *Know thyself*. You can only begin to know yourself through silence. Continue to watch yourself, even in your dreams. On waking recall a dream if you can. Reflect on it and record it (always do this in the present tense, as though it is happening now). Relax and wait for your intuition to discern its meaning for you. For now, take this thought with you into sleep:
Through Silence we are guided along many pathways to God, ever upwards to the highest realisation any human can have: the knowledge that he or she is Divine.

END OF DAY CHECK LIST:

- **LET GO**
- **OBSERVE YOURSELF**
- **TRUST YOUR INTUITION**
- **CHOOSE WISELY**

Chapter 5
The Pathway of Self-Knowing

Whether you know it or not, you are on a journey of discovery which will eventually lead you to the Lighted Way, the Way of Revelation. But how often do you walk, your eyes downcast, and focus on the little things of life? Or do you sometimes raise your gaze to the night sky and wonder at the worlds beyond worlds that you see there, tiny points of light that in truth are brighter than a thousand suns? Do you pause then and ask your self: Who am I exactly? And what am I doing here?
Oh, how easy it is to forget! (The Lighted Way)

The path ahead is one laid down by you alone. No one else can direct you for you are the light on your own path. You light the way.

To retreat is to step back and gain a clearer view of yourself. How well do think you know yourself? Are you able to see yourself as others see you? Can you view yourself objectively – is this possible, do you think?

In your relations with others are you able to be yourself - or do you lead a double life? By that I don't mean are you having an affair or working as an undercover agent, but how much is your inner life separate from what you do in the world? Are you able to be true to yourself regardless of who else is around?

And what of the 'Inner You" - how much time do you spend on your inner life? Think about this for a moment. Do you even have an inner life?

'Who am I?' and 'Why am I here?' are questions that have occupied human beings for aeons. Self-discovery is a search for meaning and purpose beyond the obvious and mundane.

I wonder what 'being spiritual' means to you. In one sense it is so simple a thing: it is nothing other than being true to yourself. However, this is much harder to achieve than 'simple' would suggest for most of us are raised to be true to other people's ideas about 'who' we should be. Expectations from our parents, our teachers, our culture and religion, although often well-meant, all help to create a false identity which eventually must be examined and dismantled. Remember that there has never been another you and there never will be. To be yourself is the essence of spirituality; it is your precious gift to the world.

Spiritual people are those who no longer see themselves as the centre of the universe; their thinking and actions demonstrate an awareness of others being as important as, and equal to, themselves. Such people strive to make the world a better place. They may not meditate or believe in angels, or even God, but they do contribute in a positive way to our civilization, as artists, scientists, educators, activists and the like. Being 'spiritual' isn't just about religion or even New Age beliefs and practices. It involves being true to our hearts and living out our highest ideals.

'Being spiritual' rests on a profound understanding of ourselves and others, and places real value on an inner identity that is eternal rather than transitory. Success is then no longer measured by wealth, power or even how long we live but by how well we live in relation to others.

In order to do this we need to establish a place of peace within ourselves. This point of focus – or Centre - is fundamental to our retreat. It is the home of our Undying Self. Whenever we enter retreat we also return home.

Our Soul is divine perfection, our closest experience of God, but it has great difficulty in expressing itself through us. Being Light, its vibrations are much higher than those of the body and it has to penetrate not only the heaviness of a physical body but the dense substance of emotional desire. Not least, it has to 'see through' all the illusions created by the human mind, both personally and collectively.

Contact with our Soul is often, at best, spasmodic. We can be aligned and receptive to the soul's influence one minute and the next we have lost it. It is rather like trying to tune in to a radio station, to a programme that we very much want to hear, yet the signal is poor or intermittent.

Moving our point of focus, by an act of will, from the dense vibrations of a mind constantly occupied with memories and desires to a vibrationally higher place definitely helps to maintain and strengthen soul contact, as does any altruistic activity. When we do this we become a bridge between two worlds, the human and the divine.

Let me share a story with you. For many years I was haunted by the symbol 'X'. It would appear to me wherever I went - as twigs crossed on a path, aircraft trails in the sky, or random road-signs that caught my eye. 'X' would flash before my eyes, sometimes at night as I surrendered to sleep. Something was trying to get my attention. I began to fear this 'X', believing it to be a warning of some kind, a portent. Later I reasoned that it might represent a kiss or a blessing instead! I invested many kinds of meaning in this 'X' but none satisfied my curiosity. Then one day I was given a book that I had wanted for some time.[1] I opened it at random and there at once was the persistent symbol once more.

The text that followed explained that 'X' is formed by two 'open' triangles, one ascending (representing the mountain of aspiration or human consciousness) and one descending

to meet it (which is Divine consciousness). The Divine and human can only meet and blend at this point, the mountain peak, if you like.
This symbol was I realised, urging me to 'raise myself up' beyond every difficulty and to hold my attention high at all times, whatever challenges faced me.

An interesting point then emerged. It is said that just as we find it difficult to raise our vibrations to meet the Divine, so too the Masters and Guides have difficulty lowering their vibrations to meet us. In going to the Mountain we are of great service to the Divine.

---

[1](See *'Talking with Angels'* by Gitta Mallasz) Published by Daimon Verlag 2006

Day 9
Morning Practice (as before)

9
Acceptance

How well you know yourself!
Why then do you avoid your own Presence?
You know exactly where you stand,
There is nothing you can hide from yourself any more.
So, do not walk away
Be the centre of your own attention!
Practise Acceptance on yourself
Practise Patience
Practise Love

The Morning Resolve
As we spend more time in Silence, we start to see ourselves more clearly. Suddenly we are faced with the truth - the nice and the not so nice – and this is often why so many people avoid time alone; not because of loneliness but because they are afraid of what they might discover. But once we have acknowledged the existence of our soul as our guide we cannot turn away from our self. There is no hiding and no going back.

We have all made up stories about ourselves to justify how we live. We may try to fool ourselves or others but we can never outwit our own soul.

Soul, the Watcher, knows exactly who we are and what we do - and why. Yet it is also infinitely patient and accepting. It observes our life in the world with unconditional love and compassion.

Today we have an opportunity to express three wonderful soul qualities: Acceptance, Patience and Love. Let's begin with ourselves. Let's begin by seeing ourselves exactly as we are, human beings, with nothing hidden. Let us accept the truth of our own flawed humanity. This is important – it is the foundation of love. We need to acknowledge our human weaknesses and difficulties in order to love others. This takes practice so we also need patience.

Right now, *patiently* observe your own struggling, weary self, doing its best from day to day. Look back on all the tests you have already endured and overcome in this lifetime and love yourself all the more for it.

When the climb to the mountain top gets tough and you develop spiritual vertigo and say 'I've had enough, I can't go on,' remember that you are the Mountain, you are your own Path. There is no turning away from yourself. This takes some practice but resolve to stay just where you are without running away. Be your own faithful companion. Accept yourself and it will be so much easier to accept others. You will feel more understanding, more loving, knowing that they too struggle and have tests to endure.

Closing
As you prepare for the day ahead be conscious of living the Life of your Soul in very practical, everyday ways. With each breath be more aware of that Undying Life. Let each moment count!

The Evening Review / Journal notes and reading
Today's message is perfect material for our Evening Review. Each one, properly undertaken, involves a high level of honesty and self-watching. It also requires a good deal of acceptance, patience and compassion. As before then, look back on the day as a detached observer, neither shrinking from human errors nor basking in self-acclaim!

Dealing with unfinished business, coming to terms with yourself and making peace in this way is always beneficial to sleep. Be your own patient companion.

END OF DAY CHECK LIST:

- **BE YOUR OWN PATIENT COMPANION**
- **ACCEPT THE NICE AND THE NOT SO NICE!**
- **LOVE YOURSELF FOR IT ALL**

Day 10
Morning Practice (as before)

10
Who Am I?

Do not hide from your humanity, neither from your greatest nor meanest;
Instead raise it up.
Waste no time on self-analysis for this tells you nothing of
Who you are
Instead, take to the Mountain and from your high place,
See the sun rise on your valleys and riverbeds alike.
See yourself, laid bare.

The Morning Resolve

This is really a continuation of yesterday's message of acceptance and observation. As hinted previously, when you begin the process of self-watching in earnest you will find many things you would rather ignore! The more time spent in your High Place the more light becomes available to you - and the easier it is to see into the dark places. Everything in this world is based on opposites that eventually must be reconciled – high, low, light, dark, joy and sorrow, and so on. Being human we all have a 'base life.' This lower aspect of humanity will demonstrate as cruelty, greed, jealousy, pride, competitiveness, suspicion, and selfishness of all kinds. These are all examples of 'glamour' or illusion created by emotional desires. Glamour is a mist or fog that prevents us from seeing life as it is. This means that we create our own false reality and are often oblivious of the real world veiled by the mist. This message invites us to recognise the many sides of our character, including the glamours, and then raise it all up to the light of the soul: the nice and the not so nice! Just like yesterday's message this is another exercise in recognition and acceptance.

The most important question we can ever ask is *Who am I?*
Ask yourself this, not once but often; not casually but deeply.
Who am I?
Let's remember that the personality (or ego) is our soul's means of contact with physical life. It is also what adds colour to the life and makes us so interesting! Remember too that our soul, caught up in form, has difficulty in piercing the illusions inherent in it. We may try to analyse and explain away our glamours but this will not fundamentally change them. Instead, as this message suggests, let us hold everything up to the clear light and reality of our soul on its own plane. We then begin to understand Who We Are.
Resolve today to ask this question often: *Who Am I?*

Take a balanced and realistic view of yourself. Note some of the things you like about yourself, your achievements – successes of the spirit. Things such as honesty, determination, gentleness, openness, strength, caring, an ability to listen, generosity, humility, a sense of humour, integrity. Think how you may make a difference, even in the smallest of ways.

Closing
Be the Watcher today. Watch yourself with great interest; be observant but not neurotic! The secret is detachment. Stay at a little distance. Calmly and honestly observe your thoughts, words and actions. Compassion is the key - make no judgment on yourself and you will be less likely to judge others.

The Evening Review / Journal notes and reading

Have you noticed how the best novelists demonstrate a keen understanding of human behaviour? They get inside their characters' heads and unflinchingly reveal a variety of human glamours and illusions. Such writers observe – no doubt in themselves too – the greatest and meanest of human achievement but often with such humour and compassion that we relate sympathetically to their characters. The writer is both involved and detached at the same time.

From your High Place, look back unselectively on your day. Imagine yourself as the main character in a story you have created. Today is just one chapter in that story. Get outside the narrative and review (literally 'see again') today's episode. Allow thoughts, motivations and choices to surface at random without censoring them.

Notice the highs and lows of the day – again review everything without judgment, regret, blame or congratulations. Add in some compassion and a good measure of humour. Smile at yourself! Which glamours have you identified with today? Try making a list and see how many you can add over the next few days! Then notice the lessons learned and those that still need more attention. Spend only as much time as you need. Once again, accept that you are human – one who is doing their best - and finally let go.

END OF DAY CHECK LIST:

- **GO TO YOUR HIGH PLACE**
- **ACCEPT *ALL* THAT YOU SEE!**
- **RAISE IT ALL UP**
- **SMILE AT YOUR HUMANITY!**

Day 11
Morning Practice

11
Detachment

Like a good watchman stand guard over your own life.
Be ever watchful;
Guard your errant mind, guard careless words.
You have a tendency to over-react, due to a lack of detachment.
You are called more than ever now to avoid personal drama,
Even though you may find great pleasure in it!
Stay at a little distance always:
Notice what hurts, what angers or what unsettles and look for the lesson.
Is this a lesson in patience, in humility, in forgiveness or courage?
Or is it simply a call to love more?
Ask: What in this situation would my Soul do?

The Morning Resolve

Detachment. Some people are not comfortable with this word because they confuse it with aloofness or indifference. The problem is this: detachment can sometimes sound smug and needs to be balanced with compassion and understanding. We must never criticise ourselves or anyone else for suffering the pain of attachment or forget the appalling suffering people experience - an old man dying of starvation or a mother grieving for a lost child.

Attachment comes in many forms - attachment to possessions, to people, to ideas, to our physical appearance or health, to what other people think of us. Ask yourself: how attached am I to other people's opinion of me? Do I need their approval or their praise? We are only attached to approval and praise because these reinforce our sense of self-worth. And we dislike criticism because our already fragile self-worth is under attack and likely to be destroyed.

We are not free from these attachments because we learned at an early age that physical appearance and success matter and that love and approval are not always given without conditions!

Detachment is a precious jewel in a treasury of spiritual techniques. To 'keep your attention high,' as we did just now, is a wise and useful practice and certainly helps to develop a habit of detachment. Like the Soul in 'Return to the Mountain' (page 11), try watching your thoughts as he watched his passing memories. Quietly observe them with no hint of criticism, regret or blame. (This is difficult, it cannot be said too often, and takes much practice!)

In the original message the last line was *Ask: What in this situation would A Master do?*
It occurred to me that for the purposes of this book I should change Master to Soul; in fact I had a strong inner urge to do so. I understand the reason for this: our first Master is our Soul, our direct link with the Divine. A Master works through the soul and can only rely on us once we have a well established soul contact. This means hearing and acting upon the Voice of our Soul.

In order to do this we must be vigilant and take responsibility for our every thought, word and action. Perfect material for our Morning Resolve! We all know those split second moments of temptation before we open our mouths to speak – when we have a last chance to pull back from some drama or other, and measure our words before they do harm. In that brief moment we can consider the consequences of reacting according to our whim. We always know when something is wrong; when we should be silent and let the moment pass. We also know the fleeting satisfaction of gossip, criticism or revenge! Although we know that our soul wouldn't indulge, we also have free will and so choose, sometimes wisely, sometimes not. Only by being a good watchman can we see the challenges we face. Let us resolve to be the Watchman today.

Closing
The Mountain exercise will be very useful today. Return to the Mountain whenever you sense that you may be 'thrown' a challenge. As yesterday, be watchful and prepared. When in doubt always ask: *What would my Soul do?*

The Evening Review / Journal notes and reading
Look back on your day and notice when you have been unsettled or drawn into a drama of some kind. Have you reacted in haste or responded thoughtfully? Have there been occasions when you have given in to careless words, despite the guidance of the 'still, small voice' within?
Can you recall times when you have 'lived the life of your soul'?
Even in your sleep you can be the detached observer. Lucid dreaming is when you are able to recognise that you are asleep and dreaming and direct the course of the dream. Practised often during waking hours detachment sharpens our awareness and eventually continues as conscious or lucid dreaming.

I would like to close with this beautiful quotation from Sai Baba:
Everyone must make their exit someday - that moment should not be one of anguish; one must depart with a smile and a bow. In order to accomplish that, a lot of preparation is necessary. Leaving all that has been accomplished and accumulated during a long lifetime is a very hard task. So prepare for it from now, by discarding attachment to one thing after another. You see many things in your dreams, and you may even acquire power and position. When you awaken, you do not cry over the loss of those, even though they were very real and gave you real joy and satisfaction during your dream. You tell yourself, "It was just a dream" and move on with life! What prevents you from treating with similar nonchalance, all the possessions you gather during the waking state? Cultivate that attitude and depart with a

smile, when the curtain is drawn!

END OF DAY CHECK LIST:

- **STAND GUARD**
- **NOTICE WHAT UNSETTLES YOU**
- **WHAT IS THE LESSON?**
- **ASK: WHAT WOULD MY SOUL DO?**

Day 12
Morning Practice

12
Open Your Mind

We ask you to examine your mind.
Notice how often you close your door to new ideas or beliefs.

Open ...

Change the mental filter from time to time
And consider what is of most value to you. Do this with calm
appraisal
Not a passionate defence of what you hold most dear.

The Morning Resolve
One of our greatest challenges is to acquire freedom of thought; to recognise and question those subtle attitudes and thought forms that were formed in infancy (through our parents and teachers) and that still affect our thinking in adult years. Conditioning is something that none of us can escape from; indeed, those of us who are parents or teachers would do well to acknowledge how much we may have conditioned others in our care, however subtly. I believe that our current education system does little more to encourage independent thought than it did fifty years ago.

You may think that you are very broad-minded, open-minded even. Yet all of us have our prejudices. It may just be that you have a thing about people called Vanessa or Tom because those names remind you of some bad experience in the past. Or perhaps you turn up your nose at people who drive '4 by 4s' or who eat white bread. Or believe that everyone on benefits is a scrounger. We all indulge our little snobberies from time to time. Prejudice can be subtle. It may be something as insignificant as not trusting women with blonde hair or men with moustaches. Prejudice always prevents us from seeing people and things as they really are.

A friend and I once decided that we would take an honest look at our own prejudices. It was sometimes amusing - but mostly horrifying - to discover just how judgmental we are. Prejudice – or pre-judging – is a major glamour based on criticism and judgment. Prejudice leads not only to arguments but to war.
Let's pause now and reflect upon our own prejudices; some we have been raised with, others we have developed out of our own experiences.

Now consider the many influences there are on your body: your physical inheritance, your genetic patterning and how these have influenced your appearance or your health.
Notice the way you think and feel and speak; how you relate to others and the way you express yourself in the world; your social heritage – your own racial and cultural background, education and religious or political patterning; the ideas and beliefs and expectations that condition your life.

You may also care to consider other influences, such as previous lifetimes that have affected the life you live today; or the effects of the planets on your personality or the 7 Rays of Life if you are familiar with them.

All of these are 'conditions' that form a particular identity that appears at first glance to be the real you. Our task therefore is to stand back from these influences and to continually review our beliefs and strongly held opinions. Your resolve today might simply be to 'think again.'

Closing

As we close our morning 'sitting' a word about discernment: *Don't believe everything you think!* How many times have you heard this said? There are at least two books and one song with this title. It's always good to de-clutter the mind from time to time and review our long-held beliefs. This allows room for new concepts. It's also beneficial to separate fact from fiction and exercise discernment when it comes to new or unfamiliar ideas. To keep an open mind is great, a friend of mine used to say, provided your brains don't fall out. Discernment and an open mind go hand in hand.

The Evening Review / Journal notes and reading

Have you learned something new today? Has anything happened to cause you to re-think or expand your opinions and values? Have you learned anything new about yourself? How tolerant have you been of other people, especially those you may disagree with? What do you most dislike in others? It is often said that those things we dislike most are a reflection in some way or other of our own nature. Often at quite a subtle level this statement is uncannily true.

To continue an argument with yourself or anyone else is not conducive to sleep so as you lay down your arms – literally! - put aside all arguments, offer them up and enjoy the peace of a quiet mind. To sleep on a question invariably brings new and useful insights in the morning.

END OF DAY CHECK LIST:

- **NOTICE WHEN YOUR MIND IS CLOSED**
- **OPEN YOUR MIND TO INCLUDE SOMETHING NEW**
- **NOTICE ANY BELIEFS YOU ARE STRONGLY ATTACHED TO**

- **WHAT DO YOU DISLIKE MOST IN OTHERS?**
- **THINK AGAIN!**

Day 13
Morning Practice

13
Observe

What you so dislike in others you now observe in yourself.
So it is always.

So, continue to observe your habits
And, where necessary, show yourself another way.
Consider this week to be a model for the rest of your time on earth.
Live out your life's ideals in this one week
And see how much you can achieve!

The Morning Resolve

What a wonderful message this is. We all know the saying 'I've seen another side to you.' In life there is another side to everything for we live in a world of opposites, light and dark being one example of this duality.

The human being is said to be a bridge between spirit and matter, a soul that evolves through its physical counterpart, the personality. (See page 46). As souls we radiate light but where there is light (on the earthly plane at least) there is also a shadow. In Jungian psychology the 'shadow self' represents the unconscious or dark side of our nature, that which lies beyond our consciousness and which our conscious self does not recognise.

Interestingly, according to Jung the shadow's instinctive nature is prone to projection and will turn a personal weakness into some perceived shortcoming in someone else. (Jung, however, also maintained that this 'reservoir of human darkness' was not simply negative but also 'the seat of creativity').

The Ageless Wisdom teachings refer to this shadow self as the Dweller on the Threshold. The Dweller is said to be the sum total of all our instinctual tendencies, inherited illusions, glamours and wrong attitudes: in fact, all those personality traits that remain unconquered and uncontrolled over many, many lifetimes. The Dweller then is all that a human being is, apart from his inner spiritual self. Once the personality self is fully developed and there is real contact with the Inner Life or Soul there comes a point where the highly developed personality becomes, as it were, an entity: the Dweller on the Threshold. Then the Angel of the Presence, sometimes called the Solar Angel or Soul) and the Dweller stand face to face and the battle between the pairs of opposites begins. Eventually, the light of the personal self diminishes and gives way to the greater light of the Angel or Soul. I do not want to dwell too long on this here – please forgive the unintended pun – but will return to the subject in the next chapter (See Chapter 6: Discipleship).

The main thing is that we have an opportunity to create very different circumstances for ourselves by intending to live differently. It seems that the prospect of death can motivate us to make the most of what we have now, to improve our relationships, make a difference to other people's lives, be more creative, and enjoy the little things that we always took for granted. But why wait for death? Why wait for old age? Why regret later what we might have achieved now? NOW is the time of your life! So, in this Morning Resolve, ponder on those things that are important to you – your values, your innermost dreams – and be true to yourself. Live this day as though it were your last!

Closing

Draw your Morning Practice to a close, inspired by the day ahead – a potential turning point in your life. No matter what is going on around you may you remain peaceful and resolved. See yourself as you are rather than being too concerned with how others are. Watch yourself with honesty and even perhaps with a little amusement!

The Evening Review / Journal notes and reading
Looking back at the day how often have others been a mirror for you? If you have been tempted to blame or criticise what has this taught you about your own nature?

Has there been any turning point, a sense of renewal (however small)? Each moment is a fresh start, even now as you prepare for sleep.

END OF DAY CHECK LIST

- **SEE OTHERS AS A MIRROR**
- **WHAT DO THEY SHOW YOU?**
- **SEE TODAY AS A FRESH START**
- **NOW IS THE TIME OF YOUR LIFE!**
- **LIVE THIS DAY AS THOUGH IT WERE YOUR LAST!**

Day 14
Morning Practice

14
Let Go

When silent sitting is a struggle it is because you cling to your mind.
Why are you so afraid?
Let go.
Do you think you will lose your mind and drown in the Ocean of Awareness?
How can this be when you are already that Ocean?

The Morning Resolve
As your little mind grows quiet you enter a greater pool of consciousness. This may at first seem unfamiliar, a place where there is no time, no before, no after. None of the usual limitations we are accustomed to. Yet this is our Home, a place we started off from, a State of Perfect Peace. When we die we lose our body, we lose our mind (not to go mad but to

find a new freedom without their restrictions). We return to that State of Perfect Peace. Yet we are afraid to let go, to go deeper ... to go home. Resolve then to practise letting go a little more in every moment, every situation. Let go.

Closing
When thoughts crowd in to your time of 'silent sitting' notice how your body reacts and tightens. This is rather like learning to swim. If you tense up and forget to breathe you will sink. Continue to breathe, knowing that you are breathing and simply acknowledge each passing thought as you might watch clouds passing across the sun. Return to your High Place. Let go a little more with each breath. Your thoughts may be reminding you that you have a difficult day ahead or that you are fed up with sitting here when you could be enjoying breakfast or answering the phone. Just nod politely and return to your breathing. Now is Home! These few moments of quiet following sleep will set the tone for the new day. Take a few moments during the day to come home.

The Evening Review / Journal notes and reading
In deep sleep we go Home and enter the Ocean of Awareness, although we have no recall of it on waking. Unless we are very aware we lose sight of home during our daily activities. 'Noticing' draws us back home where we are only aware, however fleetingly, of this one moment.

Reflecting on the day which has not yet ended, have there been moments when you have 'come home'? Come home now. If sleep does not come readily make a list – even a mental list – of people needing help or healing. In your quiet place call on divine assistance and focus on each one in turn, asking that each may be well, happy and free from suffering. Of course you may like to use words of your own choice but don't forget to include yourself at the end.

END OF DAY CHECKLIST

- **LET GO!**
- **NOW IS HOME**
- **COME HOME**

Day 15
Morning Practice

15
Come Home!

You hear the ticking of the clock and it reminds you
That there is little time to fulfil your purpose.
Remember your duty to stay awake, difficult as that is
When you are drugged with anxiety and exhaustion.
Remember also that you are doing your best –
You have not entirely failed Us!
Discipline yourself but do not be harsh.
Bring yourself lovingly into line; call yourself home!
You have already crossed windswept plains.
You are well equipped to do so and to reach the Master's heart.

The Morning Resolve

Since we are told that time does not exist and we have all eternity, why the rush? Here is the paradox. Each time we come into incarnation our soul enters a contract to fulfil certain ends, not necessarily consciously remembered but sensed intuitively.

As we mature and evolve we are drawn more and more to a purpose that is beyond selfish desire, to some goal that is inspired directly by the soul. The conflict arises when our outer life impinges on the inner life and we get side-tracked by worldly ambition, fear and weariness.

But notice the oblique humour here: 'You have not entirely failed Us …'

You have already achieved so much, come so far and

discipline does not have to be harsh. As before, resolve to call yourself home, lovingly, to a state of awareness.

Closing
In these final moments of your morning retreat practise being very relaxed and awake and aware. Call yourself home at times throughout the day.

The Evening Review / Journal notes and reading
In recalling the day, look for times when you have brought yourself lovingly into line. In these moments perhaps you will have sensed some higher purpose in your life. It is when we are relaxed, awake and aware that we receive impressions from our soul.
Remind yourself that you have done your best and that you are well equipped to achieve all you came to do!

END OF DAY CHECK LIST

- **CALL YOURSELF HOME**
- **BE RELAXED, AWAKE AND AWARE**
- **THERE IS LITTLE TIME – YET ALL ETERNITY**
- **YOU ARE DOING YOUR BEST**

Day 16
Morning Practice

16
Truth

There are two things that humanity seeks –
Pleasure and answers to the great mysteries of life.
A disciple no longer seeks pleasure but finds it on a higher
octave as joy,
Through service and self-knowing.
Few there are who willingly stand vigil to themselves,
Unflinching in the truth this brings.

The Morning Resolve
Truth! Suddenly the focus shifts from self-centred satisfaction to finding meaning and purpose elsewhere. Through self-discovery the seeds of discipleship and service are sown and the next two pathways are created.

Here we have a further reminder of the Soul's purpose. As we proceed along the Path of Awakening or Self-Knowing the mundane things that once caught our attention no longer do so and we turn more to things of a more subtle nature – the great mysteries of life. The light of our soul reveals increasingly more of the Truth we are seeking.

To stand vigil to ourselves and fearlessly witness the best and the worst in our nature is not easy as we have found. Yet there is much to be gained.

Resolve then, above all else, to continue to observe yourself at all times – to see the underlying motive behind your words and actions – but always with compassion.

Be watching always for truth.

Closing
As we close remember also to look for pleasure in the little things. Begin and end your day with gratitude.

The Evening Review / Journal notes and reading
On this final evening of Self-Knowing let us prepare for our new pathway: The Pathway of Discipleship. As a soul you will find great pleasure in the small things of life, in Nature, in the company of friends and loved ones, in a simple meal and in your own Presence. Look back on today to recall such moments of gratitude and offer your thanks for another day well lived.

END OF DAY CHECK LIST

- **LOOK FOR TRUTH IN ALL THINGS, ESPECIALLY IN YOURSELF**
- **SEEK PLEASURE IN THE LITTLE THINGS OF LIFE**
- **OFFER YOUR THANKS**

Chapter 6
The Pathway of Discipleship

My self-forgetting is my moment of glory

This Pathway causes more hesitation than any other, perhaps due to a misunderstanding of the word disciple. Most people think of a disciple as a follower of a spiritual teacher or guru. The word originates from the Latin *discipulus*, a pupil or one in training. I remember clearly my Latin teacher's command when our attention wandered – quite often in my case - away from the lesson to the playing fields outside: *Discipuli – pictoram spectate! (Pupils, look at the blackboard!).*

Whenever we begin something new, whether this be a foreign language, car maintenance or meditation, we require a teacher. In the case of meditation some would disagree and affirm that since this is a natural human activity it needs no instruction. Indeed left to its own devices the awakened personality is instinctively drawn to a practice of self-reflection through the intervention of its Master, the soul.

Some people, especially those who have been influenced by religious doctrine as children, are uncomfortable with the idea of being a follower and with the discipline implied. However, for aspirants to discipleship in the true sense, all spiritual training is self initiated and comes initially from our own soul. So too does discipline - along with a number of necessary tests and trials! A disciple then *willingly* follows a path, offered by the activity of his or her own soul. It is only much later after he has been tried and tested countless times that the individual's radiance increases and he is eventually spotted by a Master. (It is only by the brightness of our aura that we are recognised as potentially useful to a Master's plans. Only then can the soul in incarnation – you and I – be trusted eventually to work under the direct guidance of a Master, as true disciples).

As followers of our own soul we soon find that life around us changes. We are no longer so interested in the things of the world – in material gain or success. We enjoy the little things of life much more, the things that money cannot buy (Message 16).

A disciple chooses the higher over the lower. For some time those trivial and self-centred activities that once attracted have begun to lose their appeal. There is a growing tendency to renounce anything that no longer serves his growth and his sense of purpose. People 'fall away' quite naturally, those who are no longer of like-mind. (see Message 5). There are gradual – or even sudden - changes in life-style; changes that promote better health and choices that benefit the world at large. A disciple is aware of being in the world but not of it. He doesn't turn his back on the world but faces life with the vision of the soul.

A disciple aims for purity of body (through a simple, healthy diet), control of emotions and stability of mind.
Above all, the disciple seeks to serve and thinks inclusively rather than exclusively, knowing that we are in essence one another. It is thus that we are led eventually to the Pathway of Service.

There are many obstacles ahead of the traveller on the Pathway of Discipleship and we shall consider some of these over the next few days. One of the great disappointments for most is how quickly we can turn from feeling peaceful one day to agitated the next. You may well ask 'How can we possibly maintain a state of poise and contentment regardless of our circumstances?' One very simple way is to enjoy all your problems! This may sound facetious but it really means that you can take comfort in the fact that all obstacles on your path are helping you to grow in stature. You can think of one day's coping with a challenge as a significant triumph over fear or despair and a further step towards mastery.[1]

Fear is the greatest obstacle and the greatest of our glamours; it often highlights perceived lack and powerlessness and lies behind many negative states – jealousy, insecurity, arrogance, criticism and the like. Fear can stop us from living our lives authentically. We can recognise many of our own glamours by 'noticing,' observing ourselves, not in a neurotic but a balanced and detached way. Or perhaps more effectively by 'noticing' the things we dislike in others!

---

[1] We learn to be Masters by mastering our own problems, by putting right our own mistakes, by lifting some of humanity's burdens and forgetting ourselves. The Master did not comfort me that night, He offered me no compliments or nice platitudes. He said, in effect, the work must go on. Don't forget. Be prepared to work. Don't be deceived by circumstances. *(The Unfinished Autobiography of Alice Bailey, p. 88)*

Day 17
Morning Practice

17
Aspiration

We show you the mountains, distant, and how your heart leaps.
Soon you find yourself at the edge of a great plain and wonder:
How is it that the peaks are now not so high?
Because you are already there, Beloved!
Already there, carried by lifetimes of pain and joy,
And by your great aspiration!
Weep not, for this was ever yours.
This is no dream!
And yet greater things are for you to behold,
As your blanket of doubt falls away!

Hear Us in the silent chamber of your heart.
We come to lead you home that you may show others the Way.
You see ahead the great lineage of aspiration, a road of Infinite Light?
Rejoice in the lives of those who go before you,
And of those who follow you.
Lay all your doubts to rest and trust.

The Morning Resolve

Welcome to the Pathway of Discipleship!

This first message gives us a sense of perspective. If we like to believe we have come a very long way indeed on the road to enlightenment it serves as a reminder that there is an infinite journey ahead (a road of Infinite Light, Life Eternal) and that there are many ahead of us who lead the way. If on the other hand we doubt that we have made any progress at all we can rest assured. There are equally many who follow and for whom we act as guides. We are just 'somewhere' along the journey to Mastery.

Two things that I personally took from this message are its reassurance and promise of purpose and service - a reference to our next Pathway.

Lay all your doubts to rest and trust ... We come to lead you home that you may show others the Way.

It also reminds us of the importance of listening - with the inner ear attuned to the silence of the heart. Therefore whatever your resolve may be today, may it also include Silence, that special silence of the heart where you will gain perspective and balance.

In considering your ongoing journey you might also try this remarkably simple but powerful exercise: *If I were not afraid ...*

Write down the phrase: *If I were not afraid ...* and complete it as many times as you can. It might go something like this: *If I were not afraid I would drive on the motorway and save myself time* or *If I were not afraid I would ask my neighbour to turn the television down.* It might uncover uncomfortable emotions: *If I were not afraid I would enjoy someone else's success (and not feel a failure myself).* Or it might be something quite dramatic like: *If I were not afraid I would leave my job (or my husband/wife) and live in a community.*

This is a very non-threatening and potentially life-changing way to look at fear; it creates no pressure and simply highlights areas in your life where you hold back. You may be surprised at how limited your life is by fear; and surprised too that you suddenly feel more ready to make changes.

Closing
Allow yourself a few more minutes to rest in the silence of your heart and resolve to carry silence and peace with you throughout the day.

The Evening Review / Journal notes and reading
What has your silent observation revealed today?
Have there been moments of revelation, times when you have acted with a courage you didn't know you had? Continue to challenge yourself at intervals with the

opportunity to live a more spacious and rewarding life.
Reflect now on your path and trust in its ever-unfolding purpose. Continue your journey to the Mountain even in sleep.

END OF DAY CHECK LIST

- **LISTEN WITH YOUR HEART**
- **TRUST**
- **IF I WERE NOT AFRAID I WOULD …**

**Day 18
Morning Practice**

*18
Be Your Own Guide*

*Guide your mind and teach it to serve you.
Put your mind in training and let it reflect your will.
You will gain great pleasure from this practice and enjoy unexpected results.
Notice but do not be dismayed by the waves that disturb your quiet pool of consciousness.
All misdemeanours, all excesses of emotion, eventually give way to wisdom.*

*This is a time of incubation.
There may be much going on that you do not like, that you rail against.
You may say 'I have had enough.'
Yet there is much of which you are unaware: a stirring within you, a quickening.*

*Hold true to your purpose, steadfast in your desire to bring forth your finest work.
Take yourself to the clear light at the mountain top, whenever you feel the need.*

The Morning Resolve

This message holds the key to mastery. It is time for us to develop our will and take responsibility for our thoughts. As we have been told before and will be told again, discipline need not be harsh and it can bring unexpected success. 'Noticing' the workings of the mind and the consequent fluctuations of emotion sends a strong signal for change. We begin to 'wise up' to our addictive and unhelpful thought forms with their various chain reactions. We must never stop 'noticing' or asking 'where did this feeling come from'? Noticing helps us to gain perspective and see the bigger picture – even to question our thoughts and beliefs. This questioning is inspired by a subtle stirring of awareness and it will lead to its further ripening.

It is time to hold your awareness higher still; to stay at a little distance and patiently watch.

In this way you bring forth your finest thoughts, words and actions.

Closing

Regardless of what happens around you today, remember with gratitude the ever- evolving Life within. There is no turning back!

There is a subtle warning in this message too. Our steadfast self-observation makes us aware of our past conditioning. Let us not allow others to think for us. This is a time for Inner Guidance not for following others. No teacher, no guru, no psychic or medium can direct your life. They may, if sufficiently advanced, be able to point the way but *only to your own truth*. Be your own guide today and all your days.

The Evening Review / Journal notes and reading

Recall if you can any habitual thought forms that you have identified today. Any tendency that holds you back, that causes a disturbance in your quiet pool of consciousness. Do this without any self-criticism but rather the satisfaction of having discovered something new. Such discoveries ultimately bring freedom.

As you prepare to rest keep your awareness high and intend to guide yourself even in sleep.

END OF DAY CHECK LIST

- **GUIDE YOUR OWN MIND**
- **PATIENTLY WATCH**
- **NOTICE THE WAVES OF EMOTION**
- **KEEP YOUR AWARENESS HIGH**

Day 19
Morning Practice

19
Patience

The state of high emotion will pass.
The turbulence will settle in time.
Remember that you have within you all that you need, both now and in coming times.
Be patient, mostly with yourself.
Try to establish a routine and all will come more readily into line.
Neither neglect your body nor think too much of it.

Draw close to Nature, to the Mother.
Let go of regret and resentment.
Rest, empty handed and open hearted, that We may fill your hands and heart with grace.
We bless you always.

The Morning Resolve

This is one of my favourite messages and will often appear, selected at random, in times of need. Even if it doesn't seem pertinent for you today it also hints at coming times and will serve you well in the future. All things pass – the good and the not so good; everything moves in cycles. We are fully equipped to deal with our thoughts and emotions. As often before, this message calls for patience. Combined with a steady routine, balanced attitude to the body and time spent in Nature patience anchors us when we feel unsettled.

Resolve if nothing else to be patient, especially with yourself; patient with any negative thoughts and feelings that may arise. From your High Place you are less likely to be thrown by turbulence. Wait calmly knowing that help is at hand.

Closing

While fully anchored in the earth as the Mountain, spend a few more minutes in your High Place as the Eternal Watcher. Bring this attitude of patience into the coming day.

The Evening Review / Journal notes and reading

The Evening Review is an opportunity to unburden yourself in preparation for sleep and for a new day. What can you let go of today? Regret perhaps - things you feel you should or should not have said or done. Regret blesses us with insight and hope for tomorrow; it holds the promise of better things, right action in the future. Once acted upon regret has served its purpose and can be dropped.

So what about resentment? To re-sent means to 'feel again' (from the Latin *sentire*, to feel), usually lingering feelings of anger springing from a sense of injustice. Resentment poisons the body and mind and pollutes everything around us. Without relief it can develop into hatred and add to the sum total of destructive thought forms in the world, those that fuel terrorism and war.

Resentment shows us what we have not forgiven (from Old English forgifen literally 'given away'). It is useful – but also takes courage – to look for the underlying causes of resentment: feelings of having been overlooked, misunderstood, insulted, deceived and betrayed, and so on - things that have happened once too often. It is then wise to look for the lesson. Might you have spoken out sooner and challenged the perpetrator? Have you taken things too personally? What positive action might you now take that would help others as well as yourself? The self-growth that follows such soul-searching can bring relief in itself. Writing down your feelings is known to bring release (use your journal!). Self-love and selfless service will also bring solace and restore feelings of worth that may have been crushed. Paradoxically it is by mentally saying 'I love you' to those who have caused us resentment that eases the pain most of all. The love we send out (even through gritted teeth at first!) returns to us augmented. Even if you feel unable to try this yet, end the day with a positive affirmation about yourself. Let 'I love you' be your final thought before sleep.

END OF DAY CHECK LIST

- **YOU HAVE ALL YOU NEED**
- **BE PATIENT**
- **DRAW CLOSE TO NATURE**
- **LET GO!**
- **RECEIVE**

Day 20
Morning Practice

20

Purification

Thoughts have an instant effect on your well-being.
Your body will continue to clear when you refuse all dark thoughts – envy, malice and arrogance. All fear.
As you have been told before intoxication by fear is as powerful as any drug
But self-discipline need not be harsh.
It is a joyful response to the Soul's call –
And what can give more joy than service to the Soul and therefore to others?

Straight is the Path.
Walk lightly upon it.

Allow the old poisons to be neutralised.
Both shame and guilt are harmful to you and to others.
The world is polluted enough without them.
Allow the old wood to be burned.
Your fires of purification are beacons of hope,
so rest in their warmth
And know that, despite everything, all proceeds well.

The Morning Resolve

A perfect message to follow Patience! Retreat is a time for clearing and healing but this process cannot proceed if we continue to overload our system with poison. It is time to increase our vigilance, to take full responsibility for our thoughts – moment to moment. This practice may be undertaken cheerfully even with a sense of amusement when we see how self-absorbed and serious we can be. It is easy to spot a dark thought and just as easy to lighten it. Our resolve today is to walk lightly – to think, speak and act, not superficially but with lightness of heart.

Closing

Imagine a great bonfire warming you on a dark night. See the flames grow higher and brighter as you cast all negative thoughts, all the old wood, on the fire; a sign for you that all proceeds well.

The Evening Review / Journal notes and reading

How much lighter we feel when we have refused dark thoughts. Look back on the day and notice when you have been vigilant. Let this time before sleep be a process of letting go. Imagine again the bonfire. Alongside you is a bag of rubbish that you have collected during the day. Without opening the bag and sifting through the rubbish throw it into the flames with a sense of relief and hope for tomorrow

END OF DAY CHECK LIST

- **WALK LIGHTLY!**
- **REFUSE DARK THOUGHTS**
- **ALL PROCEEDS WELL**

Day 21
Morning Practice

21
Mastery

You are discovering the Way of the Masters.
As a young cub practises his hunting skills, overseen by the elders of the pack,
So you follow the examples shown to you by the Elders of the Race.
Likewise you are in training until, having absorbed the wisdom of Perfected Humanity,
You will stand alone, liberated from all that was, from all limitation and desire.
Is this your fear – liberation?

The Morning Resolve

This message is simple and needs little enlargement. How wonderful to remember that every day, every minute, we are in training! Today will yield many small opportunities for mastery and freedom. Watch your every response: worry, disappointment, suspicion, envy, and so on – all these can be mastered over time. Notice what unsettles you and take comfort in the knowledge that this very experience will bring you a step closer to freedom. Once more, enjoy all your difficulties! Mastery comes from the realisation of illusion; waking from the Dream that is our life on earth. A dream composed of fear, desire, and death. Remember too that your training is self-initiated and resolve today to see each moment as a lesson, a chance to see life anew.

Closing

Spend a few moments now recalling those Great Ones Who have experienced all our difficulties and more. They are always at hand to help: we have only to ask.

The Evening Review / Journal notes and reading

Looking back on the day, were there any uncomfortable moments, however trivial? If so, what were the lessons? Were there any opportunities to stand back and enjoy your difficulties, knowing that they have a purpose in the greater scheme of things? Remember again the wise adage 'sleep on it' and offer up now anything that you have as yet been unable to resolve. Trust that answers will come, as they surely will.

Finally go to your High Place and offer up a prayer yourself and for those who may need your help. You act as a transmitter of peace, healing and love for those in difficulty themselves.

END OF DAY CHECK LIST

- **YOU ARE IN TRAINING!**
- **NOTICE WHAT UNSETTLES YOU**
- **TAKE COMFORT**
- **RECOGNISE THE LESSON**

Day 22
Morning Practice

22
Solitude

Be not afraid of aloneness.
Enter it willingly, gladly; embrace its freedom!
Allow solitude to be only what it is: a necessary space for your spirit to thrive.
Are you lonely in My Presence?
How can you be alone when at your Centre
I AM?

The Morning Resolve

Loneliness is a very real human problem and a common cause of depression, especially (but not exclusively) for the elderly or infirm. It is an unnatural state because as human beings we are intended to live in relationship with other people. However, loneliness can strike no matter how many friends and family we may have around us.

Years ago during a rather bleak time of life I was shopping for greetings cards and spotted one that made me smile. I bought it for myself; it shows a cartoon figure standing on top of the world, looking somewhat surprised. All around her are stars and moons and three approaching UFOs; above her head the simple caption: *You are not alone*. It has never been taken out of its cellophane wrapper and sits at the foot of my bed as an amusing little reminder of a deep spiritual truth.

Solitude, as opposed to loneliness, is to be embraced for it is vital that we find the right balance between companionship and seclusion, between the outer and the inner life. This balance lies at the heart of our retreat. When we experience true solitude it is actually impossible to feel lonely because the sense of Presence and communion (Latin *communionem* or fellowship) is palpable. So, just as the daily practice of mastering the little things of life brings freedom so too does solitude, along with feelings of deep peace and expansiveness.

Let solitude be your resolve today; seek out brief moments even in the busiest of days for withdrawal into your Eternal Self.

Closing

As your Morning Practice ends allow your experience of your own Presence to continue into your daily activities. Enjoy the company of others but be your own companion at all times!

The Evening Review / Journal notes and reading
Withdrawing into the inner world is natural at this time of day. The best sleep comes after a gradual winding down of activity and after putting aside the things of the day in favour of quiet reflection.

Reflect on how your spirit thrives in these moments of quiet. Look back on your day and search for those little periods of calm. Were you able to maintain an inner silence when other people have been around you?

Are you able, more and more, to sense in your own company that you are not alone?

END OF DAY CHECK LIST

- **BALANCE COMPANIONSHIP WITH SOLITUDE, THE OUTER AND THE INNER**
- **BE YOUR OWN COMPANION**
- **YOU ARE NOT ALONE!**

Day 23
Morning Practice

23
Responsibility

Begin to realise where your responsibility to your Brother lies.
Awaken your own fire and continue to speak fiery words.
Fear not that these will evoke anger.
Your words awaken sleeping hearts and stir distant memories of home.
Warm others by your fire!

The Morning Resolve
Responsibility is a word that strikes dread in the heart of anyone burdened by duty and obligations. Let us look then at where our true responsibility lies:

Perhaps the most important lesson we learn is how to be 'who we are,' a unique and precious version of the Divine Source Itself.

The Pathway of Discipleship will present us with many opportunities to be true to this blueprint; to be authentic and honest so that there is no longer any gap remaining between what we think, what we say and what we do. The aim then is to act with one mind, one voice, one motivation, as it were, and such congruence is not easy to achieve (from Latin congruens: meeting together). We so often say and do things to please others, more often than not out of fear. We seek to be liked to fit in, yet the discomfort we feel from not being true to ourselves can develop over years from un-ease to disease. The various elements of our mind, body and spirit do not 'meet together' and we fall apart. Being at odds with our own nature creates such physical, emotional and mental chaos that the body eventually gives up. It is then that the Soul, no longer having a vehicle adequate to its purposes, decides (as my friend Bob liked to say): 'I'm getting out of here!'

Our first responsibility then is to be 'who we are' and we do this by awakening the Inner Fire. Fire has many qualities: for instance it can both illuminate and destroy old beliefs and patterns of behaviour. Fire is also a source of warmth, comfort and love.

Needless to say we also have a responsibility to others; to grant them the same importance, respect and care that we deserve ourselves. This responsibility grows in proportion to our soul contact. Sometimes such responsibility includes saying things others may not want to hear. We may need to go against the flow and not be swayed by the opinions of those around us. We may be called to speak from the heart in order to counter some popular though destructive belief, and to remind others to think for themselves. 'Tough love' is another example of this challenge.

With this message we have a hint of what is soon to come: the Pathway of Service.
A word of caution however! We should never interfere, or persuade, nor appear to have all the answers for clearly we do not. Indeed sometimes our silence can be as fiery as words in awakening others to the truth of themselves.

Recognise where your responsibility lies and resolve this morning to be true to yourself and respectful of others.

Closing
Enjoy these last few minutes in the company of your Soul, the one who always was, is now, and always will be. Let the inner fire burn brightly. Be who you are!

The Evening Review / Journal notes and reading
Just as we may fear solitude mistaking it for loneliness, we also fear rejection. In fact the two are inseparable – when we are true to ourselves we risk invoking jealousy, envy, criticism and anger in others simply by our choosing to stand apart. Notice how others are happy to support us when we are down, depressed and vulnerable but how that changes when we are happy, self-confident and successful. Our vulnerability creates no threat; our strength does, potentially at least. This evening notice how this applies to you too. How easy it is to support a friend in need - for one thing it gives us a sense of being valued. This does not imply that we are acting selfishly, only that our motives are so often mixed!

Notice how uncomfortable and insecure you feel – especially if you are having a difficult day yourself – when others receive good news, success, popularity, attention; all things that you could probably benefit from right now. Just notice – without feeling bad about your feelings and acknowledge your own honesty of spirit.
Now return to yourself and to the blessings that your own life path ever unfolds, however hard things may be at times.

Look back on your day and notice how you have assisted others, simply by being yourself.

END OF DAY CHECK LIST

- **BE WHO YOU ARE!**
- **NOTICE WHEN YOU ARE NOT!**
- **AWAKEN THE FIRE OF THE HEART**
- **WARM OTHERS BY YOUR LIGHT**

Day 24
Morning Practice

24
Humility

Give yourself to Me as I give Myself to you
This invocation shall be your own offering, renewed each day, to the Divine.
You place yourself now at the service of your Soul;
Of Those Who guide you;
And of your Brothers and Sisters in the lower worlds.
And remember that this is a dual invocation.
It is the Call also of the Higher to the Lower.
Give yourself to Me as I give Myself to you!
This is Our Call to you.
We give Ourselves to you in your moments of self-forgetting.
These are your moments of glory, when all self-doubt and self-seeking are put aside.
Beyond the need for praise, for thanks, for recognition, you understand
The true power of humility.
Each secret thought of love, each silent act of service is known to Us.
Be steadfast, be silent, yet be ready to speak for Us.
Be watchful and we show Ourselves to you.

The Morning Resolve

All great spiritual teachers are recognised by their humility. Such teachers speak with quiet authority and only ever seek to awaken the truth that lies already within each one of us. There is therefore a clear correspondence between the last message and this one. Let us too be recognised by our humility! May this be our resolve for today.

Your self-forgetting is your moment of glory. All self-seeking thoughts such as a desire for attention, praise and gratitude become insignificant in the light of humility. In the words of that great American writer, Ernest Hemingway: *You must be prepared to work always without applause.*

Sometimes we say we are humbled and we need to be – by acts of genuine kindness, courage and self-forgetting. We can equally be humbled by our own actions, those occasions when we act according to our Soul. Each thought of love, each silent act of service is more potent than we can possibly imagine. It is indeed those largely unseen and unselfish actions that we will one day come face to face with and marvel at their significance.

Closing

Spend a moment or two longer in your High Place; breathe the clear air of the mountain top. Silently remind yourself: *My self-forgetting is my moment of glory. In putting aside all need for thanks, for praise, for recognition, I understand the true power of humility.*

The Evening Review / Journal notes and reading

We now come to the point where two more pathways meet. The call to service grows ever louder for the follower of the Soul. The following exercise successfully completes the Pathway of Discipleship and prepares us for the next.

1. Before sleep stand in the dark[1] and offer yourself up, firstly to the Light of your Soul. Do this with the words I offer myself to You as You offer Yourself to me.

2. Offer yourself next to the highest representation of the Divine you can imagine: Guide, Master, Angelic Being or spiritual teacher. Again with these words: *I offer myself to You as You offer Yourself to me.*

3. Finally, offer yourself sincerely to humanity, to your companions in the world, all brothers and sisters, all divine regardless of whether they are known to you or not: *I offer myself to You as You offer Yourself to me.*

4. Stand a moment longer and with open hands receive the Blessing: ***I give Myself to you!***

END OF DAY CHECK LIST

- **SERVE SILENTLY, UNSEEN & IN SELF-FORGETTING**
- **THESE ARE YOUR MOMENTS OF GLORY**
- **I GIVE MYSELF TO YOU AS YOU GIVE YOURSELF TO ME**

---

[1] You can equally do this exercise lying down if preferred.

Chapter 7
The Pathway of Service

All that I am and all that I have belongs to others, not myself.
Alice A. Bailey: Discipleship in the New Age (1)

If you are looking for happiness you have arrived at the right place for it is often said that the happiest people in the world are those who serve. Indeed, what we know instinctively can now be backed up by science. Altruism has been a subject of research at The Greater Good Science Centre, University of California. The true meaning of altruism is a selfless concern for the welfare of others and the action taken to improve it. It has been found that giving to charity, for example, activates areas of the brain associated with pleasure. Some scientists believe that altruism may trigger the release of endorphins, naturally occurring opiate-like substances that appear to reduce pain and induce feelings of happiness.

Yes, altruism is good for you! Volunteers have been found to have generally improved health (even in cases of chronic illness) and are less likely to suffer from depression. Older people who care for others are significantly less likely to die. There are many other benefits, many known to us, including the fact that generosity tends to be contagious. Studies suggest that kindness is often rewarded and one of my favourite quotations illustrates this: *'To those who give shall be given' so that they can give again.*[1] (We often use this to promote our work in 'The Extra Guest' charity.)[2]

There are some who dislike the word service, often those who were given unreasonable responsibilities at a young age and were robbed of childhood's freedom. Service is a reminder of duty and servitude. But in true service there is no duty involved, only satisfaction and pleasure. *Voluntary* service is the result of creativity and it is creativity that builds our culture. It may be that your particular line of service is humanitarian, or through more overtly creative work – art, literature or music; alternatively you might take a more logical and scientific approach. All these are creative activities: service includes anything that creates a better and more beautiful life for all.

Jane Swarbrick is a very gifted music teacher who runs community choirs in the North of England. Her choirs are inclusive so there is no age limit and all are welcome regardless of their ability or health status. They provide therapy and enjoyment for everyone, including the infirm and their carers, and the tremendous response Jane receives bears out the claim that singing is good for the health. I happened to comment one day that what she does is an excellent example of service work; however, she replied simply: 'But I don't think of it like that.'
And I know what she means. Service arises *naturally* from what we do best. Jane loves what she does and so does everyone else - and they all benefit greatly.

Service can also be an unexpected result of suffering and hardship. Jo Berry, co-founder of Building Bridges for Peace is a wonderful example of someone who has chosen to triumph over a tragic personal loss and use the wisdom she gained in service to the world. When an IRA bomb killed her father, Sir Anthony Berry MP, in 1984 Jo had a choice. She could either harbour anger and revenge towards those responsible for his death or seek understanding instead. Her extraordinary journey not only brought peace to her own life but has resulted in her becoming a much loved and respected ambassador for world peace and reconciliation. She met, befriended and now works with Patrick Magee, the very man who planted the bomb that took her father's life. Together they work internationally to put an end to violence, and to promote peace and reconciliation through empathy and understanding.[3]

It is by using the very stuff of our own lives in service to others that our culture is built. It may not always result in some great mission but instead something equally important like being a good parent or caring for a neighbour. If you are unsure about your own line of service remember that both service and creativity bring fulfilment. Do whatever you love – there is no age limit for fulfilment! What fascinated you as a child? What made time stand still? It is sad that some people never find fulfilment or, in later years, live vicariously through others. For many though old age can bring a resurgence of purpose, an opportunity for adventure and seeking out new experiences.

Service begins wherever you are. Even infirmity is no bar to helping others with our focussed thoughts and prayers (see Message 26 Evening Review). As the American psychic and healer Edgar Cayce advised: *Why worry when you can pray?*

The Inner Journey – the one we undertake now on retreat – will bring all the experience and wisdom needed. Service will not necessarily make you wealthy but you will receive gifts of the spirit more precious than anything you can imagine. You may not receive thanks or acknowledgment but as Message 24 reminds us our moments of glory are in our self-forgetting. It will result in a relationship with yourself that more than compensates for any partnership you may lack but long for, and will only enhance those that you already have. Service brings a regard for yourself and for others that will lead you directly to the last of the pathways, Love.

---

[1] Quotation from *Reflective Meditation on Attracting Money for Hierarchical Purposes* (Discipleship in the New Age (2) by Alice A. Bailey).

[2] The Extra Guest: Food for All end-hunger charity promoting 'ethical dining.' www.theextraguest.com

[3] Jo Berry and Patrick Magee were featured in a BBC programme, Everyman: Facing the Enemy. www.buildingbridgesforpeace.org

Day 25
Morning Practice

25
Inspiration

Breathe!
Inspire!
This is your calling –
Inspire in your Brothers and Sisters a true love of life
And of one another.
Draw from Us, Who work as One,
The courage, wisdom and steadfast Presence of the One Life.

The Morning Resolve
How good it is to inspire others; to encourage them when they are overcome by self-doubt. Encourage[1] means to hearten – to give strength when needed. 'I believe in you' is something we all need to hear at times when our self-belief falters. In fact it was all thanks to my friend, Lyn Harvey, who had faith in me that I began this book and thanks to more friends still that I persevered in finishing it.

I cannot stress enough the importance of perseverance. This message offers us courage, wisdom and *steadfast Presence*, all qualities of the Soul. So be steadfast! Too many people abandon perfectly sound ideas and projects at the first sign of difficulty and say, 'Oh well, it wasn't meant to be' or 'It is what it is' simply because things haven't immediately succeeded: they lack perseverance, imagination and flexibility.

A Chinese friend of mine has always wanted to write a book but since living in England for many years she has almost lost much of her mother tongue.
'I'm neither good enough in Chinese or English,' she explained, 'I'm stuck somewhere in the middle.'
I was convinced however that she would make an excellent

writer with a fascinating and poignant story to tell about life in a new culture. I felt full of enthusiasm on her behalf. My instinct was that she should write first in Chinese. Her experiences since coming to Europe would be of great interest to other Chinese people living here. 'You can do it,' I said, 'in fact, you must do it!'

There was a certain sadness about her and even though she has a happy home life, something was missing. I knew her spirit had to be expressed. 'Read in Chinese everyday,' I suggested, 'novels, newspapers, anything. It will soon come back.'

Her face lit up as she began to see possibilities ahead of her. She is now planning to attend a writing group to get her started.

Inspire means to breathe life into something. We might begin then by remembering to breathe, consciously. Resolve to breathe life into your own plans and projects today and watch for opportunities to inspire and encourage others. In this way you create a climate of optimism and likely achievement.

Closing
A true love of life comes from an appreciation of the miracle of life itself. Spend a few moments silently reflecting on the wonder of your own life. Remember always to 'love the life you live and live the life you love.'[2]

The Evening Review / Journal notes and reading
Please join me now to reflect on moments in your day when you have been inspired. And other moments when you have acted on an impulse to inspire others.

Next recall those who have inspired you throughout in your life and how they have helped to shape your destiny.

Finally, before sleep, imagine yourself at the end of a long and fruitful life, at peace with this thought: *I have done all I came to do and perhaps a little more.*

Remember this: whatever is your Soul's desire, you can achieve it!

---

[1] from the Latin cor (heart or inner strength)
[2] *Love the life you live; live the life you love* (often attributed to Bob Marley but arguably inspired by a lyric by Muddy Waters and Willie Dixon).

END OF DAY CHECK LIST

- **WHO OR WHAT INSPIRES YOU?**
- **BE STEADFAST**
- **INSPIRE OTHERS**
- **LOVE THE LIFE YOU LIVE**
- **LIVE THE LIFE YOU LOVE**

Day 26
Morning Practice

26
Healing

It is not with your hands alone that you heal.
It is your task to remind others of the Subtle Worlds.
But how may you do this when you forget the reality of those worlds yourself?
Stay awake and awaken others!
In forgetting you lose an opportunity to serve.
Light the way for your Brothers' and Sisters' safe return!
How else may you arrive at the feet of the Beloved?
How else will you reach the Master's Heart?

The Morning Resolve
Your Morning Resolve is an opportunity to enter the real world: the Undying Life of your Soul. This is also the experience of NOW.
It is only through our soul and its connection to higher realms that we heal and are healed. We heal with our

thoughts, prayers, words and touch. Even looking into another's eyes with loving intent can heal.

Let us resolve to stay awake today to the reality of our Undying Life. The Beloved is that Undying Self and through its grace we eventually have access to the Great Teachers and Masters of Wisdom. May we light the way for all with whom we come into contact!

Closing
Rest and breathe. Spend a few moments more in the company of your Soul and receive all that you need for the day ahead.

The Evening Review / Journal notes and reading
To end your day I am going to suggest a simple practice that will be of great benefit to you and others. After reflecting on the day that is ending and having made peace with yourself and others wherever possible, we turn now to healing as service.

Distant Healing and prayers are offered with the intention to relieve suffering (see Message 35: *Work to alleviate suffering, as I work to alleviate yours*).
When we are ill, in pain or overcome by anxiety it can be difficult to find refuge and access the Inner Healer. It is then that we benefit from those who can mediate on our behalf. Years ago when I was in hospital I found it impossible to 'tune in' but a friend sent me a card in which she had written the message: 'I ask, dear sister, on your behalf.' I have never forgotten her kindness and trusted that healing would come even though my own connection felt so fragile. Healing therefore is service par excellence. In case you have any doubts about the power and efficacy of Healing Prayer, do have a look at Larry Dossey's website. Dr. Dossey is known internationally for his work integrating spirituality and healthcare.[1]
In all my years as a healer I have never been so convinced as I

am now of the power of prayer and the practice of 'distant' healing. What impresses me most is its simplicity: it requires only a minute or two of focussed attention and a sincere intent to help. It is an act of service both to the individual in need and to the Divine Healers called upon to intercede. The simplicity of this practice rests in its reliance on Love. Regardless of preparation exercises and techniques - grounding, protection and the like – unless the healer is a ready channel for Love, nothing of consequence will be achieved. When Love alone is the intention miracles can and do happen! A focussed thought of Love will cross barriers of time and distance and will touch the minds and hearts of those prayed for. Love is the great link between all forms of life and most certainly between the healer and the one who receives. Healing is a partnership in which all receive healing, all benefit.

Although it isn't my intention to tell you how to heal – everyone will have their own method – I will describe how I work and set out a few guidelines which I hope will be helpful:

- Firstly it is useful to have a notebook dedicated to healing prayers, a place to enter the names of those who have requested help.
- It is 'healing etiquette' firstly to receive permission from those who require healing. When this is not possible I make a petition to the individual's soul and proceed in a 'Thy Will Be Done' fashion. We can never 'send' healing to anyone in any case. It is simply an offering from one soul to another, the healer being the instrument for the highest available source of healing power.
- Healing into Dying is an especially privileged form of service. Our healing prayers are always beneficial both during the dying process and after transition. These are not offered to hold individuals back but with the intention of assisting them on their journey.

- Evening is often the best time to practise this form of healing. It seems to encourage deep relaxation in the healer and restful sleep to follow. Begin with your usual preparation for meditation: relax, breathe and go to your 'High Place.'
- Make a conscious connection with the highest source of healing you can envision – this may be an angel, guide or some spiritual figure that you relate strongly to.
- Ask that each person on your list, yourself included, may receive the healing that they need, in mind, body and spirit. A simple request - based on a Buddhist prayer to relieve suffering - might be: *May all be well, may all be happy, may all be free from suffering.*
- You may find that your hands begin to tingle or grow warm just as though the person were physically present. I then hold my hand/s over each name in turn and quietly say a few words of healing, whatever comes to mind in the moment.
- If you have a very long list to go through and little time available you may ask that everyone on the list receive healing. (I do personally find it beneficial to say each name aloud if nothing else but others may not find this necessary.)
- It is often useful to make a few notes during or after the Healing session. Any recorded information may be very useful to the individual prayed for and allows him or her to play an active part in the healing process.
- At the end of your Healing session ask for healing for yourself if you have not already done so. Always close with thanks to those healing guide/s who have overseen the session.

---

[1]*Healing Words: The Power of Prayer and the Practice of Medicine*
Larry Dossey 1993 (Published by Harper Collins)

END OF DAY CHECK LIST

- **RECALL THE REALITY OF THE SUBTLE WORLD**
- **STAY AWAKE TO AWAKEN OTHERS**
- **LIGHT THE WAY**
- **WORK TO ALLEVIATE SUFFERING**

Day 27
Morning Practice

27
Understanding

Develop a deep understanding of others.
Cultivate respect and a care-full attitude.
Let them be as interesting as you are to yourself.
Be to others as We are to you: lovingly observe
and never interfere.

The Morning Resolve

Understanding arises from careful (care-full) observation, whether this is of oneself or another person. In either case when we begin to understand the human condition we develop empathy, the ability to imagine walking in another's shoes. This ability profoundly alters the way we respond to other people. We are far less likely to judge, to criticise, or to feel superior. We may not agree with what others think and do but we can at least acknowledge that were we living their life we might not be so very different.

Are we also able to allow others to make their own choices? Can we resist interfering even though we may think we have all the answers? Instead, can we continue to observe, understand and empathise and only offer counsel if invited to do so?

How we love to air our opinions! How little we listen, waiting instead for a chance to talk about ourselves. *Active* listening is a form of noticing, an act of regard for others.

Remember that we too are lovingly and patiently observed by those in the Subtle Worlds.
Let us resolve to listen with care: firstly to the Inner Voice. When we are attuned to the Inner Life we will find it easier to know how and when to assist others.

Closing
Spend a few moments more in silence. Observe yourself. Observe the 'watcher.' Notice that you are being noticed!

The Evening Review / Journal notes and reading
Looking back on today, have others been as interesting to you as you are to yourself? Perhaps they have been even more interesting! Have you noticed a difference in your relationship with others when you have listened with care? Have you been aware of an increase in intuition for example? Active listening is a healing tool, one that builds trust and deeper understanding. It is a form of unconditional love.

When you have completed your Review, take time for your Distant Healing / Healing Prayer practice. Make contact with your own Soul and envision the highest possible source of Divine Healing available to you in service to others. Remember also that you are lovingly observed and guided at all times yet always free to make your own choices.

END OF DAY CHECK LIST

- **BE CARE-FULL**
- **OBSERVE**
- **LISTEN**
- **UNDERSTAND**
- **EMPATHISE**

Day 28
Morning Practice

28
Let your voice be heard!

Let your voice be heard and your hands ready.
I AM HERE!
Be prepared day and night to serve.
You may be called upon at any time ...

The Morning Resolve

How often do you say 'I am here for you' and what does that really mean? Does it mean 'I am here for you as long as I'm not busy or tired or watching my favourite TV programme?' Or are you prepared to 'be here' even if it's rather inconvenient right now?

Those Who watch and guide in the *real* world of the Soul are always 'here' for us. 'Let Your Voice be Heard' is Their invitation to us to use our voice as a healing tool (see also Messages 23, 24 and 35). Whenever we are present and attuned to the world of the Soul we need never doubt that the right words will come; they always do and often have a profound effect on those who hear them. Today we are summoned to speak and to act as required. Let us be prepared to hear the Call, whether from our own Soul, the Guides on the Inner Planes or our brothers and sisters in the world - and resolve to be ready!

Closing

Be attuned to the 'still, small voice' within you. Carry your quiet time in the *real* world into your daily activities and discern whether silence or words are appropriate. Remember that you never work alone; *I AM HERE* is a reminder that Those in the *real* world are always there to prompt when needed.

The Evening Review / Journal notes and reading

Even in our sleep we may be called to serve on the Inner Planes. During periods of deep dreamless sleep it is said that we enter a place of learning (called The Halls of Learning and the Halls of Wisdom, depending on how far our Soul has advanced). Sometimes we are taken to people and places requiring assistance, healing and even rescue work. These occasions are mostly not remembered except occasionally as lucid dreams. You may, like me, remember such dreams where we are called upon to help – or be helped. One example I would like to share with you came from my son. He was in his late teens when he awoke one morning from a particularly strange and moving experience:

I found myself hovering in space above the Earth and looking down over England. I had no awareness of my body at this point and rapidly scrolled down the globe in a straight line until I found myself over Africa. As I approached South Africa I zoomed in suddenly and at the same time seemed to come down into my body once more.

I found myself in a dark empty space and was immediately conscious of a little girl on my back, her arms clinging tightly around my neck. I could feel the weight of her as she struggled to hold on. It was very, very real, unlike any normal dream. I felt like I might choke as she tried to pull herself up a little higher.

Even though she was behind me I could see her clearly – a little blonde haired girl of around five or six. I could observe myself at the same time and could both see and feel from a different perspective. All the while I knew I must keep very still and stay calm in order to help her.

Suddenly I woke up and got ready for college. Later I switched on the television to watch the news. There was a news item about a young girl who had been kidnapped and murdered by a white man in Pretoria, South Africa. The photo on the screen was of a blonde haired girl, exactly the same as the one in my 'dream.'

I have never forgotten this experience and know I never shall.

Nor is this something I will ever forget. My own sense is that my son was called to help and comfort the terrified child who had found herself in a dark and lonely place and perhaps didn't realise that she had died. His role was rather like that of a spiritual paramedic and a sense of urgency took him to exactly the right place. I imagine that teams of divine helpers on 'the other side of Life' would then take her to the Light where she would be cared for. This story really does underline for me how we must be prepared to serve day and night. Before sleep you may like to make a simple dedication to this effect: *I am here!*

Complete your Evening Review in the usual way with healing prayers for yourself and others.

END OF DAY CHECK LIST

- **BE PREPARED**
- **LET YOUR VOICE BE HEARD**
- **I AM HERE!**

Day 29
Morning Practice

29
Joy

The world awaits:
Bring forth your own offerings and assist Us in Our work.
We are ever patient but as more time passes so does the
opportunity to achieve your finest work.
Trust your Path!
Follow it and you will be rich beyond your imagining.
This, We know, is what you crave, a joy that cannot be spoken of.
So where is the joy?
Serve not for duty but for joy.

The Morning Resolve
In case yesterday's message sounded a little daunting 'Joy' reminds us that we are only called to serve when we are ready and able. Even if we are a little inconvenienced we need only remember that 'it's all my time anyway'! When we trust this, opportunities for service will always arise if not always in the way we have envisaged.

Service doesn't have to be some grand mission that will bring accolades and grateful thanks. It may even go unnoticed, by the world at least. In the *real* world it will always be seen and known.

Today resolve to follow the Pathway of Service wherever it may lead you. Find joy in the little things of life.

Closing
Spend a few moments more in your silent place as you reflect on your life's purpose. Sadly fulfilment may not always come directly from work we are paid to do but for a soul committed to his or her life path creative opportunities will always arise elsewhere. *Trust* your Path!

The Evening Review / Journal notes and reading
Recall moments in your day when you have experienced unexpected pleasure and fulfilment in small things. Reflect with gratitude on these moments.

Now consider your own special gifts and talents. How might these be employed to achieve your finest work?

Continue with your Evening Review in the usual way, ending with Distant Healing and Prayers for yourself and others.

END OF DAY CHECK LIST

- **TRUST**
- **ALL TIME IS MINE**
- **FIND JOY IN THE LITTLE THINGS OF LIFE**

Day 30
Morning Practice

30
Manifestation

*The principle desire of your Soul
(if desire may be used in this way) must be to serve.
Perhaps this then will throw light on the question of manifestation.
Consider the desire to manifest money or good health.
Money, health, opportunity – but to what end?
The will to serve manifests all that is necessary to serve the Soul's Plan.
'Consider the lilies of the field'!
Let service be your goal, my Brothers and Sisters.
Your desire to serve your own Soul will invoke every opportunity needed for this task.
Simply trust!*

*Affirm daily your intent to serve.
May you wonder at the humility and gratitude that this invokes in you.
Offer yourself wholeheartedly to this task.
Only then will your prayers for 'more this' or 'more that' be forgotten.*
Ask only for what is needed and know that your request is already granted.
Such freedom, such unimaginable abundance, awaits those who awaken to this truth.

The Morning Resolve

Trust can never be repeated enough for doubt and anxiety are ever part of the human condition: we worry that may not have enough money to survive or support our families or sufficient good health to live a purposeful life. These are very real and understandable anxieties. Look around you: people are losing their jobs, their homes; you may even be one of them. Look further and see many more who are dying from lack of food in a world of plenty. Who would have thought that in modern America, England and other European cities and towns, Food Banks would be set up for those who can no longer manage to feed themselves and their families? And yet strangely enough we also witness the generosity of ordinary people who are more interested in giving than getting. This is true service.

We have a dilemma however: our culture is so rooted in greed and the desire for 'more' that we constantly seek out whatever we believe will make us feel secure. 'Enough' just isn't enough in a world where success is measured by one's economic or celebrity status. Sadly even the New Age has its own professional gurus who promote excess in the name of abundance. There are even those, I am told, who preach that to consort with the poor only brings down our own vibration and therefore does not serve us. Can you believe this - and how appallingly ignorant this is of the Laws of Life!

Abundance is both desirable and possible *for all* - but only in a world where sharing and human kindness has replaced selfishness.

The simple life can have a great appeal for those who are not seduced by 'more.' Living simply doesn't mean living a deprived life at all. Jose Mujica, president of Uruguay, is a wonderful role model for simplicity. He has rejected the luxurious presidential home offered to him and opts to live in a modest farmhouse instead. He and his wife work the land themselves and his simple lifestyle - that includes donating about 90% of his salary to charity - has led him to be known as the poorest president in the world. He is probably the richest man on earth viewed from the perspective of the heart.

Now and again it is useful to ask ourselves: *what exactly do I need – as opposed to what do I want?* Reflect on this now for a while and try to answer it truthfully. For most of us the honest answer will be that we need far less than we thought and surprisingly there is real freedom in knowing this.

But returning to trust: how many times do we doubt ourselves and our purpose in life? Just as unquestioning self-belief can prove foolish and dangerous, self-doubt can be equally trying. In my case self-doubt stopped me from writing this book. Thoughts like *Who on earth would read it?* or *Would it be good enough?* held me up. And then after several false starts it took someone I really trusted to insist – to the point of tears - that it would be very useful to others before I finally committed to finish it. Interesting, isn't it? It was the sincerity of her emotion, her feelings, which got through to me more than any words. Once I was persuaded of its potential usefulness all I needed was follow it through – to do my part and trust. If my motivation was fuelled by a desire to serve then the needed opportunities would be invoked. And indeed they were – but that is another story.

Our resolve today must surely be this, to live the simple life with all the freedom this brings: *My desire to serve will provide me with all that I need in body, mind and spirit.*

Closing
Let us complete our Morning Practice by appreciating the gift of our own life. This will include our Life Story to date and all that has brought us to this point.

The Evening Review / Journal notes and reading
Before you begin your review, stand in the dark and with eyes open look for little points of light within it. Don't worry if this doesn't happen for you! Breathe – and know that you are breathing. Feel how alive you are. Say 'thank you' (aloud if you can) for your life. Recognise the wonder and mystery of this life, and all life.

Next offer yourself as a gift to the Divine (to your Soul, and to whatever power or Presence you perceive as greater than yourself). Do this knowing that *All that I am and all that I have belongs to others, not myself.*

As you continue your review in the usual way know also that opportunities await you to make a real difference to the world around you.

END OF DAY CHECK LIST

- **ASK ONLY FOR WHAT IS NEEDED**
- **TRUST**
- **YOUR REQUEST IS GRANTED**
- **THANK YOU!**

Day 31
Morning Practice

31
Reassurance

This is not what you expected to hear from Us today.
You have asked, (begged even!) for some sign, some reassurance concerning your work in the world.
You desire proof, something to inspire confidence and initiate action.
This is your proof: your love of humanity; your need over all else to serve.
Humility is your protection -
Go forward in step with your own dear Soul
Your heart awaits your Brother's call.

I AM HERE!

The Morning Resolve

We are all grateful for signs and hints that 'inspire confidence and initiate action' although these can sometimes be missed. Today let us resolve to 'notice' a little more than usual so that inspiration doesn't pass us by. Sometimes we don't recognise the signs till later and only then understand their relevance.

For years my dream was to become a published writer. I had already written a collection of short stories, was two thirds through a novel and had begun two books based on my retreat work. I just lacked the necessary motivation and confidence to go on. There is something rather scary, for me at least, in being 'out there,' exposing one's thoughts and feelings publically – and permanently. It's my version of stage fright. There is sometimes a daunting feeling of responsibility for writers too: supposing we get it wrong or influence others badly?

Eventually I asked myself: *Why is it so important to you to be published?* Without hesitation the answer came. In moving forward the only condition was to be in step with my soul. Writing, I knew, was a means of reaching out to a much wider audience as a healer and inspirational force. I have always recognised the healing power of the voice and know that this applies equally to the written word, in both factual and imaginative work. But how would I achieve my goal?

Even though I am technologically inept I am also aware of the enormous spiritual benefits and contribution to our culture of the 'World Wide Web.' It was in fact through using the Internet that I first made contact with Lynne Ralph, founder and editor of *Inspirational Storytellers*. Lynne liked my work and kindly responded with "I hope you will say yes to being one of our Inspirational Storytellers.....I would like to help spread your words around the world ..."

Be in step with your Soul and all will fall into line! This rule really does work for all of us, whatever line of service we are involved in. The deal is simply to be the voice of your Soul – not to become famous or wealthy (as the ego may wish!), although these too may be consequences if in the interest of the Soul's work and its furtherance.

Both love of humanity and humility guard us from the culs de sac of ambition and keep us on track.

When seeking reassurance simply reflect on your love for others and your sincere desire to serve. As your Resolve today may you *go forward in step with your own dear Soul!*

Closing

Rest silently for a few minutes more and attune yourself to the Call of your Soul. Ponder on your own gifts and how they may be used in service to others.

When you struggle to find answers, unsure of the best course of action, always return to your Centre. There sits your Teacher, the Heart of Love.

The Evening Review / Journal notes and reading

Trace your footsteps back through today and see where you may have wandered off the pathway in your thoughts, words and actions. Acknowledge also the times when you followed the direction of your own Soul. In those inspiring words of Alice A. Bailey (from A Treatise on White Magic) we may wander down the by-paths of ambition, of self-interest and material enchantment, but the lapse will be but brief. Nothing in heaven or hell, on earth or elsewhere can prevent the progress of the man who ... has heard, even if only once, the clarion call of his own soul.

END OF DAY CHECK LIST

- **LOVE IS YOUR PROOF AND REASSURANCE**
- **HEAR YOUR BROTHER'S CALL**
- **GO FORWARD IN STEP WITH YOUR SOUL**
- **I AM HERE**

Day 32
Morning Practice

32
Brotherhood

You remember your promise to serve the Brotherhood of Man?
Your anxieties about your coming work are understood.
The instability you now experience will lessen as you become aware of the nature of group service.
You do not work alone.
We are, as you have been told, never far.

Often, though, you are unable to recognise your own worth objectively.
Others may sometimes deflect you – with intent – from that recognition; blinding you with their own good deeds and achievements.
Wisely and silently, you applaud their skill but, know this –

Yours is the way of love.
You will know through love; see through love; heal through love.
Your devotion to your Brother will reward you with gifts of the spirit as yet unseen.

The Morning Resolve

We may, if we are fortunate, have some distant memory of our Soul's purpose. Remembered or not, our Soul has a contract to fulfil in this life, one that is altruistic in nature and founded in love. As touched on in Chapter 1, young children often display a natural capacity for empathy and a desire to help others. I remember my own fumbling attempts to care for and demonstrate love for those around me – nothing gave quite as much pleasure and satisfaction as this! Much later, when studying German at school I came across the phrase 'die Bruderschaft der Menschen' (Brotherhood of Man) in some 'A' level text. I felt instantly and inexplicably elated; in that brief moment time stood still and nothing else mattered. Those words brought a revelation that transported me to a higher level of my being, like a grand piece of music, and I shall never forget it. It was both a distant memory and a hint of things to come.

We may also as children have a definite sense of vocation (which I did not have however). Such certainty may come about through the recognition of some burgeoning talent, encouraged by parents and teachers, or simply an inner knowing. There is no doubt then about the future life path or service – it is just there, waiting to be taken up. For many of us though the future is not so clear. We may also be deterred by a lack of self-confidence.

We rarely see ourselves as we are and tend to have either too much or too little self-belief, resulting on the one hand in superiority and on the other inferiority. Both are illusory. If we could but understand our value as equal to others' there would be no place in our world for envy or competition.

It seems appropriate to share a supplementary Message on this theme, one not included in the set of Guidance Cards: You serve despite those failings that you inwardly treasure! Intolerance is balanced by compassion, mean thoughts by magnanimous action. *You serve through your humanness not despite it. You do well to examine yourself but do you always see the greater picture? Deny your virtues no more.*

The truth is that *we are all gifted* and although we may be the first to appreciate talents in others we so often overlook our own.

It is however our sincere desire to 'help' that acts as a powerful invocation that will eventually match up our own skills, however latent, with some external requirement. We need only to remember that service does not necessarily mean some grand 'Mission' - humility counts for so much more in the life of the Soul!

For many of us responsibility weighs heavy yet lightens when we realise that we do not work alone. We are only responsible for our small part in a much bigger Plan that involves the whole of humanity. Such a Plan is overseen by Those Teachers and Guides (Masters) who have evolved ahead of us. Our willingness to serve helps not only our brothers and sisters in the world but the Masters too who rely on our involvement to initiate the major changes necessary for humanity's evolution.

This period of our evolution is, and will be, increasingly influenced by group consciousness and the recognition that humanity is one family. Whatever activity we choose now as individuals will be linked to the work of a group and motivated by a concern for others. The power of the group will enhance and stimulate our capacity for service work more and more as we begin to demonstrate unity out of diversity. Far greater goals can be reached by a unified group than by individuals working alone. We are each responsible for using our own gifts to the full and thus contribute to betterment and evolution of life on Planet Earth.

To sum up this rather long message, it is in the end only Love that confers true self-worth, purpose - and the realisation that we are inseparable from one another. There are in this message elements of all the other pathways: Silence, Self-Knowing, Discipleship and Service.
Through sincere service we can be trusted and blessed with gifts of the spirit previously denied us: gifts to be used selflessly for the benefit of others.

Let us now reflect on our own place within the human family. This is a truly mind-expanding exercise. Regardless of our differences such as race, beliefs, gender, character, age and our precious individuality, may we resolve today to see each person we encounter as just another 'me.'

Closing
Relax deeply in the Silence of your Soul. We are now being led closer to the Pathway of Love. As Souls we have no gender – thus 'Brother' and 'Sister' are interchangeable, the one word having no more importance than the other. Experience yourself if you can as devoid of gender, simply a Soul that inhabits a male or female body for this lifetime. Each man or woman or child that you meet today is another Soul, another you.

The Evening Review / Journal notes and reading
We are now at the end of the Pathway of Service and only days away from the end of our 40 day retreat. This last message has given us much to reflect on, not least that all the

previous pathways lead into and form part of the Way of Love. Service in particular increases our ability to love – which in turn stimulates further our desire to serve.

This Evening Review offers you an opportunity to release any burdens - anxieties and doubts - that slow down your progress. Look back on today, and particularly with regard to your relationship with others. Notice where you have felt an easy rapport and where you have not. Where it has been difficult to relate to an individual, go back now in your imagination and see him or her as one who suffers, as you sometimes suffer, with difficulties and challenges perhaps greater than your own. See him or her as 'another you.'

Turn to yourself now and weigh up your own heart. Does it feel heavy or light? An open heart, you will realise, is a light heart. A heavy heart is one that is closed or partially closed.
In your Healing Prayers ask for assistance in opening and freeing your own heart. Healing will often be most effective at night during sleep and will prepare you for the next stage of your journey.

The heart must be lighter than a feather in order to enter the next phase of our journey. We must let go of any deep resentments and past bitterness that make our hearts 'heavy' and seize the opportunity to move on and grow amidst all the pain and trauma. To remain open-hearted in the face of where we are wounded, vulnerable to others, and not seeing clearly, is a courageous thing to do – truly the test of a strong and open heart.
(Lynne Kirwan, Psychological Astrologer)

END OF DAY CHECK LIST

- **YOU DO NOT WORK ALONE**
- **YOURS IS THE WAY OF LOVE**
- **YOU ARE JUST ANOTHER ME**

Chapter 8
Departing: The Pathway of Love

Stand naked in My Love and I give you a New Cloth,
a New Life.
(from Message no. 40: A New Life)

Life is full of arrivals and departures, beginnings and endings. We began our retreat with Silence and will end it thus too, aware that all approaches to the Mountain converge in this final Pathway, Love. Within each pathway also may be found all others. Let us recall T.S. Eliot's famous lines from his *Four Quartets* – lines that symbolise Divinity's awareness of Itself through Its descent and exploration of matter:

We shall not cease from exploration
And the end of all our exploring
Will be to arrive where we started
And know the place for the first time.

Love and The Seven Rays of Life
The Ageless Wisdom teaches that Life in all its forms is conditioned by seven great streams of energy or Rays. These are known as the Seven Rays of Life and their various qualities influence human life on many levels. In fact every department of existence is said to be 'coloured' by a combination of these rays.

The Seven Rays govern our Soul, Personality, Mental, Astral and Physical bodies and to some extent explain our uniqueness as human beings as well as the many differences between us. The Rays lend colour to the whole person: our Soul will be on a certain ray whereas our personality may be influenced by a different one altogether. Our mental body may be governed by yet another and the astral/emotional and physical bodies by another still.

Certainly, some knowledge of the Rays can help us to appreciate the complexity of human nature and understand ourselves and others a little better. Although no one ray is better or more 'spiritual' than another, the fact is that we will naturally feel a closer affinity with some - those similar to our own - than with others.

It is not my intention to discuss the Rays in any depth in this book,[1] save to mention that there are three major 'Rays of Aspect': 1 (Divine Will or Power), 2 (Love-Wisdom) and 3 (Intelligence and Adaptability) and four minor 'Rays of Attribute': 4 (Harmony through Conflict), 5 (Concrete Science or Knowledge), 6 (Idealism or Devotion) and 7 (Ceremonial Order and Magic).

It is Ray 2, however, (the Ray of Love-Wisdom) that concerns us here on the Pathway of Love.

Our own Solar System is said to be governed by Ray 2; one that provides the overriding influence on Planet Earth and the reason perhaps why we view our Creator as a God of Love. The other six rays all influence life on earth but are sub-rays of this basic ray, Love-Wisdom.

Love, from a spiritual perspective, is an attractive force; the binding, unifying force that holds together all of creation. Love sustains all life, not just yours and mine but the planets and the oceans and all that is seen and unseen; imagine it as the binding force throughout creation. Love keeps everything in harmony, from galaxies, solar systems and planets to rocks, plants, animals, human beings and their cells and atoms.

I begin with this brief outline of the Seven Rays in order to discuss the existence of a Divine Embodiment of the Love Principle, and to throw some light on the Messages that follow.

The Christ: Avatar of Love
Each of the Messages on the Pathway of Love refers to such a One. Known to the western world as the Christ, Lord of Compassion, He is both a Divine Being in His own right and representative of a Universal Principle (Love) that humanity is destined to embrace and demonstrate. The Christ is a perfected human being, an Elder Brother and senior member of the Spiritual Hierarchy – the Master of all Masters.

The Christ is not the property of the religion named after Him but belongs to all creeds, to all humanity. He is the Avatar or Teacher expected for this current cycle of human evolution by all the world's major religions, and known variously as the Messiah, Krishna, Kalki Avatar, the Imam Mahdi and Maitreya Buddha. He is also referred to as the Coming One, the World Teacher, and some would say Saviour - although this does not adequately describe His rôle. Such a Teacher has always come in response to the needs of a particular Age but never to save the world by doing our work for us. He can only help by showing us the way to a better and sustainable future – that is, through right relationships, namely justice and sharing; a way that is already being recognised and advanced by the more awakened members of the human family.

Many believe that such a Teacher is already present in the world, inspiring humanity behind the scenes.[2] The fact remains however that we live in an unjust world on an ailing planet for which we, humanity, are responsible. Millions starve in a world of plenty: this is a major crisis that threatens the stability of us all. No such Teacher can emerge until humanity has recognised and demonstrated a degree of Brotherhood and Oneness.

It is the Christ Who is our model for loving, and the 'Christ Child' who is born symbolically in our hearts as we evolve to an awakened heart. Many there are now in all departments of life who have experienced this 'birth.'[3]

It is to this end that I offer these last eight Messages – to inspire in the reader a sense of hope and expectancy and the desire to create these much needed changes and thus to hasten the emergence of the Coming One.

---

[1] More details will be found in the sequel to this book, *Fiery Love*.
[2] For further information visit www.share-international.org
[3] In esoteric terms, the 1st Initiation of five, leading to Mastery.

Day 33
Morning Practice

33
Awakening

Humanity is beginning to raise its gaze.
Raise yours also, My Brothers and Sisters and see that My Light has already come into the world.
Know that My Love awakens men's hearts.
The Christ is here!

The Morning Resolve
Do you remember the first days of our retreat when we began to 'notice'? And how we were urged (on the Pathway of Self-Knowing) to raise our gaze beyond the little things of life? Let's take this to another level now and notice ourselves at the forefront of a New World Order. Can you raise your gaze further still and notice the subtle changes - however slow these may be - that suggest a new recognition of Brotherhood, equality and justice? Do you notice around you the signs?

So much is now coming to Light: tyranny is being challenged; in the last few years we have witnessed the rise of 'people power' and the downfall of oppressive regimes around the world. Sexual abusers and corrupt financial dealers continue to be rooted out and brought to justice. Once classified information concerning the existence of UFOs is now being released.

Be aware of the power of Light and Love over darkness in your own life too. Whether you perceive this Presence of Light and Love as a great spiritual force or as a Divine Being, it hardly matters. It is the very recognition of its presence that brings hope and beneficent change.

Let us resolve to raise our gaze today and focus on the bigger picture, the greater Life.

Closing
In these last moments of your Morning Practice, feel a gentle awakening in your heart.
Allow love to be the keynote for today.

The Evening Review / Journal notes and reading
Continue to raise your gaze as you look back on the course of your day. How has love featured in your thoughts, words and interactions? What has awoken your heart?
Can we be more aware of the nature of love and understanding of what it is - and what it isn't? Human love is a very beautiful and powerful feeling but Divine Love is an impartial state of being. Perhaps we can expand our experience of 'being in love':

What about being in love with life, and with yourself? Notice what inspires your imagination, how you love to spend your time, what you look forward to most. Look around you and search out those things – those people – that fill you with joy and gratitude. Fall in love with the sunrise or the tree in your garden.

Fall in love, stay in love! 'Being in Love' is not the unstable condition rendered by romantic love – it is something sound and enduring. Our quest for 'true love' is an echo of something more profound. Deep within us we know the truth of what lies ahead of us; Eternal Life and the blending of our soul with its now perfect reflection at the end of a very long journey.

Through love we are 'Christed.' Love, we are told, must always begin with ourselves yet somehow self-love is most difficult to achieve. The more we can identify with our Eternal Self the easier it becomes for Love is of its very nature.
Our Healing Prayers ritual gives us this opportunity. It is both an act of loving kindness to ourselves and to others.
End your Evening Review with a blessing for yourself and others.

END OF DAY CHECK LIST

- **RAISE YOUR GAZE!**
- **RECOGNISE THE POWER OF LIGHT & LOVE IN THE WORLD**
- **FALL IN LOVE, STAY IN LOVE**
- **PRACTISE LOVING KINDNESS**

Day 34
Morning Practice

34
Preparation

You are here to prepare the ground on which the Great Lord's Feet will tread.
But prepare first your own ground.
Make ready your heart for His Coming and with open doors welcome Him in.
Let your heart speak aloud and announce His Approach:
He comes!
He is here!

The Morning Resolve
Today we are preparing the ground for something momentous: the universal presence of Love as we have never before known it and the consequent transformation of humanity and the planet itself. Since the last exemplar of perfect love walked the earth over 2000 years ago there is little to suggest that His teachings have been taken up by humanity at large. So, whether or not you are open to the idea that a Teacher comes for this time - as for any other in past - the need for humanity to exemplify Love is more pressing today than ever. Nothing less will save our world from destruction.

Some years ago, ahead of a period of extreme personal challenge, I received the following words near the close of a meditation: "Your tears shall water the earth on which His feet will tread." This theme has been repeated in the message above, emphasising the necessity of tilling and harrowing our own 'ground' in order to yield the best outcomes. This process (i.e. 'harrowing') is, as the word suggests, often distressing but our tears have a softening effect on our own hard ground. This softening allows our hearts to open to give and receive the love we so desire.

To 'make ready our hearts' for the universal expression of love, in the true meaning of the word, we need to understand what this means. Over the next few days I will attempt to clarify in terms of our human experience.
Most of us find it pretty impossible to love ourselves deeply, let alone anyone else – that is to say, completely and without reservation. Our human love is *part-ial,* reserved for whomever we deem worthy. Divine Love is, in contrast, totally *impartial* and proffered regardless of 'who we are and what we have done.' We have rarely, if ever, experienced that kind of 'no strings' love.

Those things that we like least about our own human nature, things we have been criticised or punished for, or that make us feel ashamed, unworthy or afraid, all keep us from feeling love-able. Yet even your most carefully guarded fears, embarrassment, weakness or selfishness are not yours alone but are inherent in every one of us.

It is the very acceptance of our selves, 'warts and all,' that develops in us an understanding of human nature and ultimately love for others. Love, expressed as compassion, flowers from our own struggling and consequent 'reconciliation of opposites' within our own nature – our 'good and bad', our love and hatred, generosity and selfishness, suffering and joy, and so on. Love arises when we feel another's pain and want to help. Love heals, makes whole.

So how each of us lives really matters. This very lifetime – even today - offers us the opportunity to heal ourselves and others. And we do this by giving and receiving love. Can we *begin* to love as we were meant to love – by seeing ourselves in *all* living beings, knowing that we are indeed one another? I believe we can.

Begin today by resolving to love yourself a little more.

Closing
Reflect on the hope that Love brings and open your heart.

The Evening Review / Journal notes and reading
Have there been occasions where a deep understanding of your own nature and others' has been called for? Such understanding is the result of careful observation – 'noticing' with the Eye of your Soul – and will often reveal the futility of blame. Errors are necessary conditions in the great experiment of life! Breaking old habits takes much time so even the smallest change must be applauded.

All this enables us to see the Love that defines our true humanity, the 'living Christ' within each one of us.

Continue your Evening Review in the usual way with the assurance that Love is the power that precipitates all healing.

END OF DAY CHECK LIST

- **PREPARE YOUR OWN GROUND**
- **FIRST LOVE YOURSELF**
- **UNDERSTANDING REVEALS THE FUTILITY OF BLAME**
- **ERRORS ARE NECESSARY CONDITIONS IN THE EXPERIMENT OF LIFE!**

Day 35
Morning Practice

35
Open your Heart

Recognise the Christ, the Ever-Loving One within you and express it.
Recognise the Christ, the Ever-Living One in one another.
Open your heart and receive Me.
Now show yourself to Me as I show Myself to you.
Open and soon you will see Me.
Make known My Presence.
Work to alleviate suffering
As I work to alleviate yours.
Be My Eyes, My Ears, My Hands,
My Voice

The Morning Resolve
As a very young child I was fascinated by the idea of God even though He was not presented to me as a very kind, loving and reasonable character. Instead he was a rather mean, critical and unforgiving one – definitely not someone I would wish to meet on a dark night. This aside, I didn't like to think that God was all alone in the universe, and had no one 'above Him.' Surely God would be lonely, out there in the cosmos with no one to talk to for the whole of eternity. This idea worried me. No wonder He wasn't very pleasant. However, I was also certain that beyond whatever we imagine God to be (in our very limited human capacity) there had to be a higher power still - and still higher and greater powers far into infinity. That belief has since been confirmed for me in my adult reading of the Ageless Wisdom as well as by science and the theory of an ever-expanding universe. Put very simply, the Logos (or God) of our planet is a reflection of the Solar Logos Who in turn is a manifestation of the unfathomable nature of the Logos at the heart of our galaxy. All this has some relevance to our theme, the Avatar

of Love, for the Christ is, as explained earlier, an expression of the 2nd Ray quality of the Logos (or God) of our Solar System.

What I failed to grasp as a child was that God is inseparable from His Creation and therefore not alone; just as we are inseparable from Him. I had projected my own feelings of loneliness and isolation onto God. If we are inseparable from something as great as God, how is it that we feel lonely? Loneliness and a sense of loss may be due to not 'fitting in' with others. We may lack companionship and long to meet someone who shares our spiritual vision. We may even feel cheated and deprived, believing that life has been wasted, that there is a soul mate out there who has evaded us, someone who will love us and make life perfect. We say we are unlucky in love.

The reality is that unless we attain a measure of self-love we shall never attract true love. And even those partners who never matched up to our vision may be the very ones who offered us a priceless gift – the opportunity to overcome illusions and grow strong in our own identity – as a Soul.

Love can often be addictive and thus likened to a drug or poison, albeit a 'sweet poison.' It can intoxicate, confuse, break hearts open - yet at the same time transform us.

How bewildering human love is! Suddenly all our assumptions and expectations are challenged for in 'true love' there can be no ownership, no attachment, no jealousy - no fear. In our quest for this love we are made vulnerable, torn apart at times by necessary *dis*-illusionment. This idea is expressed in C.S. Lewis's marvellous lines from *The Four Loves:*

To love at all is to be vulnerable. Love anything and your heart will be wrung and possibly broken. If you want to make sure of keeping it intact you must give it to no one, not even an animal.

Our quest for 'true love' is but an echo of something more profound. Again, deep within us we know the truth: it is the longing of each man and woman for the Beloved, to have union with their own soul. When we manage to love ourselves we identify with the 'living Christ' within us and sense our own immortality.

The Resolve:
Our task today is to recognise - and express - the Eternal Christ within us; to be the eyes, ears, hands and voice of Love. When we do this we also acknowledge the Christ in others and are moved to alleviate their suffering. This is love in action.

Closing
To open the heart is an on-going process. The more we open, the more we help others. The more we try to alleviate suffering, the more our hearts open and our own suffering is alleviated – and so it goes on. Open your heart now and receive the Christ's Blessing: Love.

The Evening Review / Journal notes and reading
Cast your mind back on the day and notice when it has not been easy to love. Loving, as we know, is quite different from liking because it is impartial. We cannot be expected to like everything and everyone. It is possible to love someone in essence without liking what they do or what they stand for. We can love the Christ in them, however difficult it may be to discern beyond their behaviour! Just notice.

Notice also occasions when you have been able to see, listen, touch and speak with Love. At such times you have been a Healing Presence. Let us continue this theme now as we begin our Healing Prayers.

END OF DAY CHECK LIST

- **RECOGNISE THE CHRIST WITHIN YOU**
- **RECOGNISE THE CHRIST WITHIN OTHERS**
- **ALWAYS WORK TO ALLEVIATE SUFFERING (LOVE IN ACTION)**
- **BECOME A HEALING PRESENCE**

Day 36
Morning Practice

36
Hope

Point not to yourself but to the Christ.
Neither push yourself forward nor hold yourself back.
Announce now that you are ready and blaze the trail!
Let the unknown be known and the hidden prize be seen.
The Christ is here! Are you ready?
Go with your Brother to his high place and reveal the hope that awaits him,
Eternal Life
And may your love for him hasten the Coming of the Great Lord.
Let all see His Face and touch His Hand today.

The Morning Resolve

As any healer knows we are not the initiators of healing but simply channels through which the healing force passes. We are that same channel for all things beneficent – hope, wisdom, things of beauty, things of the Soul. And especially Love - through the ordinary living out of our days on earth we are all potential transmitters of Divine Love.

This message reminds us that we are Way Showers; your life and how you live it becomes a model for others. You offer hope and your love for your 'brother' – that is to say, everyone you meet – mystically accelerates the return of the Christ.

We teach others what we most need to learn ourselves – or what we have learned through hard won experience. It is important that we see ourselves as a meeting place of the worldly and the divine. In this way we keep balance, neither rushing forward too eagerly nor timidly holding back.

Being on retreat enables us to look beneath the surface of life and lift the veil between everyday reality and the greater reality. One of the fundamental occult (i.e. hidden) truths we discover when we live the life of the Soul is that we are eternal (see also Message 37: *Blessing*).

How easy it is to be dragged down by the ways of the world: by gossip, complaining, despair and trivial chit-chat. Resolve to be a Way Shower today and by the way you live, a bringer of hope.

Closing
Spend these last few moments, poised in your High Place, the seat of Eternal Life. Ponder on the presence of the Christ in the world and the impact that His open appearance will have.

The Evening Review / Journal notes and reading
Look back at opportunities there may have been to 'show the way,' or perhaps more correctly, 'another way.'
Difficulties may arise for those with an evangelical or overly enthusiastic nature who long to share their newly found experiences or opinions with others. This can come across as interference, and extremely annoying, especially if uninvited! Being a Way Shower is often far more subtle, involving living by example – being more peaceful, attentive, understanding, empathic, loving and respectful, for instance. And quietly being a transmitter of hope.

End your Evening Review with Healing Prayers. Ask the Universal Spirit of Love, the Christ, to pour His Healing Love through you and into each person on your list. Offer your hands in service and allow them to hover over each name. Begin or end with yourself (some people like to start with themselves so that they feel better equipped for the work).

END OF DAY CHECK LIST

- **KEEP IN BALANCE**
- **LOOK BENEATH THE SURFACE OF LIFE**
- **BE A WAY SHOWER, A TRANSMITTER OF HOPE**
- **YOU ARE ETERNAL**

Day 37
Morning Practice

37
Blessing

Miss no opportunity to offer this truth:
That all are eternal; all are Divine.

Open and receive Me.
Stand naked in My Light and
Receive My blessing now.

Now offer this Blessing to all you love:
To those who are ready to be made whole in body, mind and spirit.
May they also stand naked in My Light.

Together, rest and receive My Blessing.

The Morning Resolve

This message also invites us to share its Blessing with all we love – let us make a conscious decision to bless others, silently, throughout the day.

Love *is* the miracle of Life, though we are largely blind to it and blind to the worlds upon worlds that exist beyond both our physical sight and imaginative vision. Imagine this – you and I, potential Gods in human form - beings who are involved in some great creative process that will take us all the way from our current ignorance to enlightenment.

We are all divine – and herein lies our eternal nature.

Our knowing this will help us to share this truth and help others (lost in the illusions of material life) to discover it for themselves.

We are invited to stand naked in the Christ Light – stripped of all that keeps us chained to material life; our pretensions, expectations, desires and above all, fear. True healing is to be free of these and thus made whole in every sense: in body, mind and spirit.

Closing
Rest and allow these moments of Blessing to penetrate your Soul.

The Evening Review / Journal notes and reading
As sleep approaches, use these moments to experience the Christ's Blessing once more. Remind yourself of the miracle of your own Life, of your eternal and divine nature.

Look back on occasions when you have felt 'blessed,' having gratitude for the simple things – for friendship, for moments shared, for a beautiful view or a breath of fresh air – all these make us aware of life's miracles.

Even our blunders and oversights are blessings, for without them we would make little progress. And here is the paradox: we have all eternity in which to express our divinity yet at the same time feel such urgency to advance and grow! The answer, I think, is to take each moment in our stride – to notice our own comings and goings, our rising and falling – and know that progress is assured. There may be pauses on the journey but there is no turning back.

END OF DAY CHECK LIST

- **REST AND RECEIVE THE BLESSING**
- **SILENTLY BLESS OTHERS**
- **ALL ARE ETERNAL, ALL ARE DIVINE**

Day 38
Morning Practice

38
Light

Lay down your cloth before Me; lay down your Life.
Examine its fabric, a woven record of all you have been and all you are:
Your Life's story.
See how little threads run through it of a darker shade and rougher texture,
Little flaws that create a pattern in your cloth, reminders of human weakness and pain. Observe the beauty of your cloth, and invoke Me with these words:
Show Yourself to me as I show myself to You.

Walk joyfully into the Light of the New Day.
I AM THE LIGHT
Be light in your dealings with others – not superficial but light.
Your light can penetrate the heaviest heart and the dullest mind.

Allow Me to speak through you.
Take time, five minutes, to sit with Me.
Sit in My Light and let My Words penetrate your heart and mind.

The Morning Resolve
Today's message forms part of a longer 'Meditation on Fear' (see Chapter 9)) as does Message no. 40. The 'cloth' referred to is both the temporary 'personality body' with its inevitable flaws and the Causal body itself, the beautified sheath surrounding the Soul, woven from the finest material gathered from each lifetime. As our awareness grows so too our 'cloth' becomes ever more radiant and expansive.

Once more, drawn to the Light, we are laid bare, to reveal our own humanity in all its glory – its beauty and weakness alike. As we do this we too become lighter and freer, and able to penetrate the density of our own life. We become more radiant. As we learn to live lightly we enable others to do the same.

If we take this message to heart we will find time to sit in our closing moments and absorb the words of the Divine. I am reminded here of a personal message I received around the same time. It began, somewhat playfully, but berating me for my incessant 'busyness': *If you can spare a few minutes out of your busy schedule...*

Our resolve today then is threefold: to live lightly, to 'take time' to listen and to be the Voice of the Divine.

Closing
Take time, five minutes, in the Presence of the Christ.

The Evening Review / Journal notes and reading
As you begin your Evening Review take time to appreciate your human flaws and shortcomings for even these have been your guides. Again, approach yourself gently with understanding and compassion. If ever you are weighed down with guilt over things you have done – or not done – in the past, walk in your own old shoes for a while. Remember how it felt to be you at that time. You will quickly sense your younger, less wise self and understand. This will enable you to forgive others – and what does forgiveness mean but to 'give away'?
Without the burden of guilt and blame we are free to radiate love, rather than to seek love. In giving we receive.

END OF DAY CHECK LIST

- **LIVE LIGHTLY**
- **APPRECIATE YOUR HUMAN FLAWS**
- **TAKE TIME TO LISTEN**
- **BE THE VOICE OF THE DIVINE**

Day 39
Morning Practice

39
Be My Hands

Open and receive Me.
How can you not be worthy when you are My Hands?
You are My All,
My Healing Presence.
Be My Hands today.

The Morning Resolve
This very short and simple message reminds of our purpose in the world. Whenever we doubt our value let us remember who we are, ambassadors from the Real World, assigned to create Heaven on Earth! 'Be My Hands' means that in a very general sense, no work is too trivial or demeaning. Every activity is sacred if motivated by love. When we use our hands with healing intent the little energy centres in our palms become activated. They may buzz or grow warm, even cold, depending on the energy required. Or we may feel nothing it all because only the intent is important. We become literally a Healing Presence. As we know from our Healing Prayers the person involved doesn't need to be present – time and space are no obstacle to healing.
Today then resolve to be the Hands of God.

Closing
Take time to open, time to receive. Let the full significance of this message become clear, the very fact of your Healing Presence.

The Evening Review / Journal notes and reading
This message leads perfectly into our Healing Prayer ritual. After completing your nightly Review begin to attune

yourself to the highest healing power you can imagine. In offering yourself as a Healing Presence take time to open your heart and receive. It will also be beneficial to open your hands to enable the healing force to flow through them. For me, this is the signal to begin.

Speak each name in turn quietly while holding an image of each person, if possible, in your mind. You may find that as time passes your list becomes quite long. In this case you may need to spend more or less time on each individual, according to their need.

Alternatively, some people prefer to write names on a small piece of paper and place them in a Healing box without repeating aloud or visualising them. This way, your practice will take the same time, regardless of numbers. You will, no doubt, find a practice most suited to your own requirements. Be creative and trust your own intuition!

END OF DAY CHECK LIST

- **BE THE HANDS OF GOD ON EARTH**
- **TAKE TIME TO OPEN, TIME TO RECEIVE**
- **KNOW YOURSELF AS A HEALING PRESENCE**
- **TIME AND DISTANCE ARE NOT OBSTACLES TO HEALING**

Day 40
Morning Practice

40
A New Life

Open and receive My Love.
Stand naked in My Love and I give you a New Cloth, A New Life.
Open and receive Me
And call to the souls of those who are ready to be made whole
In body, mind and spirit.
Let them also stand naked in My Love.
Together, rest and receive My Blessing.

The Morning Resolve
This 'New Life' is a fitting end to our retreat – for every moment, every hour, and every day we have the chance to be born anew. Today we stand naked in the *Love* of the Christ and are ready to receive a new 'cloth' (see Message 38). All that has come before has prepared us for this.

This 'new cloth' has been self-created in a sense – out of every moment of compassion, every thought of love. Retreat can be permanently life-changing; time spent in the company of your Soul always will be. You will see life differently, yourself differently. You will live a New Life, anchored in the eternal.

Resolve to spend time with your Soul today and every day, and live eternally!

Closing
Enjoy these closing moments of quiet and begin to feel what it is to be clothed in a 'new cloth,' and to live a New Life!

The Evening Review / Journal notes and reading
Nothing is stronger than the law in the universe, but on Earth nothing is stronger than love. 'A Matter of Life and Death,' a film by Michael Powell and Emeric Pressburger (1946)

Just as we are born anew each day, we die each night as we enter sleep. This is when the body rests and recharges while our soul, clothed in its astral body, is off on its travels. Some people are able to leave their body and travel consciously as an 'out of body experience' (OBE) – often a truly liberating and fascinating adventure. Usually however, we are unaware of falling asleep and only remember our astral journeys as dreams on waking. During periods of deepest, dreamless sleep it is said that we receive instruction and healing from higher realms and although we are normally unable to recall anything of this, we may occasionally get vague memories reflected in our dreams.

As we prepare quietly for sleep on this final evening of retreat let us again join in a simple act of love, one we are all qualified to perform: Distant Healing or Healing Prayers.

Remember always the power of intent. Since neither time nor distance ever limit healing this can also be an occasion to remember those loved ones who have passed on and who will surely benefit from our prayers.

You may well choose to continue with this practice, along with your 'resolve' and 'review,' each day. You may also like to follow up your 40 Day and 40 Night retreat with an occasional mini-retreat, a 1 or 2 day retreat where the Guidance Card Messages are selected at random.

Either way, I strongly suggest that you repeat this retreat as often as you can. Each one will be quite different – and a New Life will emerge each time, on another ascent of the Mountain. (Enlightenment is, after all, always relative, and ever unfolding). What an extraordinary and infinite journey this is for just as one mountain is climbed another comes into view!

Although this marks the end of our 40 day retreat it is not the end of the book. Now is, I believe, the time to dispel the universal human fear of death. In the next and final chapter, 'A Matter of Life and Death,' I seek to do just this.

What follows is a collection of ideas, anecdotal evidence and research (see **Appendix**) that strongly support the premise that consciousness (and love) exists independently of the body - and even beyond death itself.

END OF DAY CHECK LIST

- **LIVE A NEW LIFE, ANCHORED IN THE ETERNAL**
- **ENLIGHTENMENT IS RELATIVE, EVER-UNFOLDING**
- **BEGIN AND END EACH DAY WITH SILENCE**
- **EVERY DAY IS AS OPPORTUNITY TO BE BORN ANEW**

Chapter 9
Arriving and Departing:
A Matter of Life and Death

On the lesser mountains of the world, in the deep forests and deserts, cities, meadows, villages and streets are sown the seeds of your immortal life.
(From Sunrise on the Mountain by Julian Middleton)

"*A Matter of Life and Death* - you won't get many signing up for that one," I was warned. "Who wants to go on retreat and be reminded of death and dying?"
Each year brings a new theme for retreat and this was the latest. I did wonder myself - suppose it's true and no one will come. Suppose people do come but fall apart and have to leave. However, I needn't have worried; the weekend was fully booked and not only that, the only falling apart was with laughter. We had more fun on that retreat than on any before it!
As you will realise by now this book, like the retreat, is concerned less with death than with Life itself. When the title first came to me I was reminded of an old post-war film by the same name, a fantasy love story starring David Niven. In the film a World War 2 pilot is shot down and bails out without a parachute. Incredibly, despite circumstances that would inevitably lead to death, he is given a second chance. Whatever else the film makers had in mind, for me it

underlines the existence of the 'Other World' (as it is called in the film) and the redemptive power of love. Interestingly, scenes from this 'Other World' are shot in black and white whereas the mortal world is depicted in full colour. 'Near Death' and other 'non-ordinary' experiences, however, suggest that the reverse is true. Our physical senses are, it seems, very limited indeed compared to their non-physical counterparts, which are greatly intensified, with colours and sounds all beyond the range of our everyday impressions.

At that time I had a lot of unresolved issues around dying, not least because a certain psychic medium had chosen to tell me that I hadn't as long to live as I might think. (I hasten to add that this was not part of a reading and that the 'information' was completely unsolicited). The prediction was said to come from a well known Avatar. It is universally recognised by professional mediums that in no circumstances should such material be divulged even if it is sensed. Perhaps more importantly we might remember that for many reasons 'channelled' information should never be totally relied upon either. (It is also widely acknowledged that Avatars have far better things to do with their time and would never give notification of this kind, especially to a third party, as in this case!) However, for a while, common sense disappeared and a rather uneasy few months ensued. I became obsessed with the thought, "Supposing it's true?"

I can only say that it felt like a death sentence, delivered with such authority that it left no room for doubt. Such pronouncements, dangerous in themselves, can create powerful thought forms and had it not been for the support of some wise and loving friends, the situation might easily have sent me into a deep depression - and even initiated a self-fulfilling prophecy.

The main danger with thought forms, especially those generated by others, is that they interfere with our 'life path.' By this I mean that they can either impose unrealistic goals that flatter the ego *(you will be rich, famous, of great spiritual service, etc.)* or worse still, cause disruptions to the

Soul's chosen course *(you must leave your partner/job/home or, as in my case, planet Earth!)*. Luckily, I resolved that I wasn't going to allow someone else's ideas to control me and began instead to explore my own issues around death and dying.

I realised that I'd first begun to dwell on my own mortality at the age of nineteen when I should have been thinking more about living. Each night back then I would go to bed wondering if it might be my last. I was also beginning to have a lot of 'non-ordinary' experiences and intimations of past lives, just as I did as a child. I see now that this was all part of a gradual 'awakening.'

Fear of Death
Death in our culture is shrouded in fear. On the whole we don't think or talk about it much or if we do, quickly change the subject. Death represents the Great Unknown and Unknowable and our ideas about it are often thought forms created by religion and designed to invoke fear and keep us in order. This final chapter explores changing attitudes to death and dying through the study of anecdotal reports and research that support the view that death is not The End.

One of humanity's greatest fears is oblivion – the idea of simply not existing any more is deeply troubling. It arouses the sorrow of saying goodbye to oneself. Maybe that was my dilemma as a young woman - my not wanting to 'leave the party,' as it were. That desire to 'carry on partying' still exists, I admit, but only in the sense of wishing to love, learn and serve and to complete certain creative projects. In 'saying goodbye to ourselves,' we might remember that all we once were, all we are now, and all we shall become, echoes through eternity and that nothing is ever lost.

There is also the distress of having to leave loved-ones, of missing them and being missed (see **Bereavement and Loss**). Add to this the regret of looking back on a life half-lived, the fear of punishment for things done or not done, plus the dread of physical suffering, and we have real reason to avoid the subject of our own mortality.

How might we address some of these fears? Firstly, I would say, by remembering that the soul (the true you and me) has no fear of death; it is this part of us that 'passes over.' It is the ego or personality that dreads the prospect of obliteration - and necessarily so for this is the primitive urge to preserve life. Ego is also the part of us that is aware of its limitations. It easily feels powerless (or powerful but in an arrogant, destructive way). It is both the frightened child and the ruthless dictator, the part that is terrified to let go; the 'me' that doesn't want to die.

Yet death is often likened to birth; the Soul's re-entry into the Real World where there is freedom from the body's limitations. Birth is then viewed as the *real* death, the end of its freedom. Some witnesses describe a visible light leaving the body at the time of death and a real sensation of energy lifting off the body and flying free. I felt this sensation most definitely with my father as he took his last breath.

The process of death is also said to be far, far easier than birth, perhaps even blissful, if we can make a comparison with nearly all Near Death Experiences (NDEs) reported. One of the consistent characteristics of the NDE is the overwhelming presence of Love; a love that is indescribable since it is unlike anything previously experienced. Likewise in death there is often a sense of wonderment and peace. My own mother was radiantly happy a few days before her passing and inspired a whole ward of patients with her joy of living.

An NDE is a 'non-ordinary' experience, usually the result of some serious accident or illness. Other 'non-ordinary' events may include apparitions, out of body phenomena, astral journeying, and even, I would suggest, meditative states. It is through practices like meditation and observation (or 'noticing') that we discover – as author Richard Holmes writes - that there is no death but only *Life in all its glory; experienced in one single and equally glorious eternal moment.*[1] Such practices take us beyond our normal consciousness and show us that Life is the antecedent of existence; the cause, not the result of our physical being.

An excellent preparation for the transition we call death is to become more familiar with the life of our Soul. Time spent in the 'Real World' of the Soul reminds us that Life itself can never be destroyed - and neither, therefore, can the bonds of love we create. *Realise that the One Life pervades all forms so that there is no death, no distress, no separation.*[2]

When we discover that heaven and hell is of our own creation the fear of punishment from an angry God is replaced by personal responsibility. This means making reparation for past actions where it is due and transforming guilt and remorse into something life affirming and beneficial to others. As for physical suffering, that is more difficult, of course. Technically, actual death should be without pain. Sometimes the process may be painful and drawn out, as with birth, but in both cases modern science is increasingly more capable of controlling pain.

---

[1] *Life after Life* (Richard Holmes)
[2] *A Treatise on White Magic* (Alice A. Bailey)

Fear of Living
The real question is not whether life exists after death; the real question is whether you are alive before death.
(Osho)

Often our fear of death is superseded by a fear of living. Each day, each moment, brings us life-changing opportunities to leave the past behind and live fully in the here and now but because of memories and conditioning we may be afraid to change, or believe that change is impossible. The following Meditation was given as an antidote to fear and offers the opportunity for a New Life, one through which we are revived or resurrected (from the Latin word surgere, *to arise*). It is a slightly longer version of two Messages featured in Chapter 8. The 'cloth' referred to symbolises the sum total of our Life as a Soul. It allows us to step out of our old, outworn garment, though beautiful in its own way, into a new and more fitting cloth of Light, a New Life:

A New Life

Fear, you will recall, shrinks the very fabric of your Be-ing. Examine that fabric now. It is a woven record of all you have been and all you are. Your Life's story. Examine it now, its colour, its texture.

See how little threads run through it of a darker shade and rougher texture. Little flaws that create a pattern in your cloth: reminders of human weakness and pain. But observe the beauty of your cloth, feel it between your hands. Now invoke Me with these words:

Show Yourself to me as I show myself to You.
Now, lay down your cloth before Me. Lay down your Life.
Step, joyfully, into the Light of the New`Day.
Stand naked in My Light. I *am* the Light.

Open and receive Me,
And speak your need to Me. Your need of love, of guidance, of forgiveness or self-belief.
What is your need?
See, feel, experience *your* need.

Open and receive Me.
And as you ask it is already given. For *you are* that love, that guidance, that forgiveness. You are that self-belief.
You are that *divinity* you seek.
Silently, speak these words 3 times: *I AM THAT.*

Open and receive Me.
How can you *not* be worthy when *You* are My Hands, My Feet, My Voice? *You* are My Eyes and My Ears.
You are My All, My Healing Presence.

Open and receive My Love.
Stand naked in My Love and
I give you a New Cloth, a New Life,
A body fit for a Christ.

Open and receive Me.
And as you stand before Me, call to the souls of those who are ready to be made
Whole in body, mind and spirit.
Let them also stand naked in My Love.
Together, rest and receive My Blessing. (Pause now for several minutes)

My Brothers and Sisters, I leave you now.
And may your body, mind and spirit be filled with the Light of the One Life from Which you come and in Whose Be-ing you are eternally present.

Living a New Life
During retreat we developed certain useful attitudes such as the Morning Resolve. However, many of us are more preoccupied with making a living than making a good and

fulfilling life. An awareness of our own mortality can be the spur to live life well - and certainly preferable to regretting too late that time has been squandered. 'Living this day as if it were our last' focusses us on what is of most importance.

Some of the most common regrets expressed by the dying include:

- I lived my life to please others rather than acknowledge my own needs
- I never dared to express my feelings.
- I didn't allow myself to be happy
- I worked too hard to make time for friends

Perhaps some of these will have meaning for you as they did for me. Unhappy people are always unfulfilled. It is well known, for example, that suppressing our emotions is a major cause of physical and emotional ill-health. So is the frustration of trying to live up to others' expectations (see **Near Death Experiences: Anita Moorjani's story, *Dying to be Me***). In short, the denial of one's own individuality does not contribute to a happy and healthy life.

In my retreats I sometimes include an exercise on self-love. It is called 'If I loved Myself Enough, I would ...' I ask everyone to complete this phrase by writing down as many possibilities as come to mind. After five or ten minutes we share the results with a partner and it is always surprising how many limitations we have placed on our lives. This realisation will often act as a catalyst for change and the beginning of a New Life.

Bereavement and Loss
You have always lived; you were never born and never will die ...
Can miles truly separate us from friends? If we want to be with someone we love, aren't we there already?
There's No Such Place as Far Away (Richard Bach)

Nothing can ever prepare us for the loss of a loved one. Sometimes a long illness may precede death and, knowing the end is inevitable, we may imagine that we have already done all our grieving - just as I did with my friend, Bob. But actually we can't. The final separation comes and it may be weeks, months or even years (although rarely this long) before grief makes its impact.

Many people become stoical and try to justify their loss as 'all for the best.' They become very busy and distracted – and eventually depressed – and find themselves unable to show any emotion, especially if they have been taught to repress feelings when young. Bereavement can follow any loss – the death a relationship, a job, a way of life.

Elisabeth Kübler-Ross (1926-2004), the Swiss-American psychiatrist, is well known for her pioneering work with the dying. She developed a 5 stage model for grief (denial, anger, bargaining, depression and acceptance) and her book *On Death and Dying* contributed greatly to changing methods of care for the terminally ill as well as the bereaved.

Edgar Cayce (1877-1945), often regarded as the most gifted psychic of our time, affirmed through his teachings the continuity of life beyond death. According to Cayce, not only will we meet our loved ones after death, but our relationship with them will continue as well. He believed that those 'on the other side' are as close to us as our thoughts and one of the greatest gifts we can offer them is prayer.

I would add to this the importance of Healing into Dying. One of the greatest privileges I know is to offer healing to the dying. In so doing, we act rather like a midwife, working calmly and lovingly, to ensure their safe delivery into the next world.

Mediumship, Eye Movement Therapy, and Induced After Death Communication

It is said that the Masters of Wisdom inspired the rise of Spiritualism in the late 19th century, as a means of impressing on humanity the existence of life after death.

A good medium not only offers comfort to the bereaved but presents a good case for the continuation of life beyond the body.

In the past few years an interesting new therapy called 'Induced After-Death Communication' (IADC) has been developed out of an already scientifically validated system, 'Eye Movement Desensitisation and Reprocessing' (EMDR). Developed by Dr. Allan Botkin, IADC enables patients to spontaneously experience the presence of a deceased loved-one – rather as a medium might. Unlike bereavement approaches that focus on 'letting go' of the loved-one, the 'reconnection' established in IADC has been found to profoundly facilitate healing. (See also section on **Near Death Experiences**).

Visitations and Dreams

Visitations and communications from the deceased can often be blocked by our grief. It is quite common to find they appear in our dreams however, where we can be more easily reached. This also applies to animals that have passed. Pets and their owners can develop a real ability to communicate telepathically during their time together, so it is not unusual for our animal friends contact us this way too. Some of my own beloved friends have visited me in dreams and one little cat even appeared while I was fully awake and in need of comfort. I had nursed him through a long illness some years before and to my great surprise he arrived quite visibly one evening to tell me that it was now his turn to look after me!

My Lost Life

"Here is a test to find whether your mission on earth is finished: If you're alive, it isn't." (Richard Bach 'Adventures of a Reluctant Messiah')

Recently I began to think about another type of bereavement, what I call 'My Lost Life.' Your 'Lost Life' may include regrets about unwise choices or missed opportunities. It may cause you to look back wistfully on things you'll never have again. It is rather like the End-of-Life Review, a chance to look back on your younger, less experienced self with honesty and great understanding and compassion.

Imagine your life span has been condensed into a much shorter time. Take a look:
- Do you have some project unfinished or plans unfulfilled?
- Are there any unresolved relationships that need attention?
- Are there more things you would like to do or places to go to?
- Are there dead parts of your self to bring back to life – gifts, qualities, that you have ignored or neglected?
- Are you 'dying to be the real you'?
- Finally, remember that *now* is the time of your Life!

Now, fast-forward and imagine the end of your life, a time that has only arrived because you have achieved all you can in this life. How will you be remembered? **Can you say, 'I have done all I came to do – and a little more'?**

Trust yourself. Create the kind of self that you will be happy to live with all your life. Make the most of yourself by fanning the tiny, inner sparks of possibility into flames of achievement.
~Golda Meir

Discovering Immortality: The Long View of Life
How are we immortal? Is it through the memories we create for others or the passing on of genes? Some say that our every thought, dream, or spoken word exists in a great memory bank called the Akashic Records, a library of every human being's contribution from the beginning of time.

Edgar Cayce was said to have access to the Akashic Records and Robert Monroe, in a series of books about 'out of body' travels confirms something similar - the existence of what he calls a Mind Belt around the earth.

Although there are those adepts, especially in the East, who are said to have achieved *physical* immortality (i.e. they have mastered their physical, emotional and mental elements and overcome death), for most people immortality implies the continuation of life in another realm or as a result of rebirth.

Reincarnation
My own childhood sense of having a 'before life' led me to seek out evidence to support the theory of re-incarnation. If there is a 'before life,' I reasoned, there must logically be an 'after life' too.

American psychiatrist Dr. Brian Weiss, author of *Many Lives, Many Masters*, has published many well-documented case studies of patients who not only re-call past identities but, in so doing, make sense of current life problems and ultimately heal them. In these and many other similar studies historical details are rigorously checked to eliminate fantasy or false memory syndrome.

Such studies confirm both the Ageless Wisdom teachings and those of the East regarding the evolution of consciousness and the progress of the Soul from one life to another.

Dr. Weiss' patients also often describe, in remarkably similar ways, an 'inter-life' state (i.e. life after death and before rebirth) during which they (the soul) would undertake a Life Review. This review would enable the individual to understand the particular lessons offered in that lifetime. They would also experience their every past action and its effect on others, both positive and negative. This, it seems, is how we learn to modify our future behaviour and become harmless in our dealings with others.

There would then follow a merging with Light, or sense of Oneness, where the learning process continues, often in the company of Masters or Guides. At some point a 'separation' would ensue as the soul prepares for a new life.

Regression, it seems, can sometimes occur spontaneously, as a flash memory or a dream. We may even experience 'progression,' that is to say find ourselves viewing a number of possible future lives. Progression usually includes a combination of our hopes, memories, precognition and, as in dreams, symbolism. Like any story we create it bypasses the logical mind and arises from the creative subconscious.

Some years ago I had a post-meditation experience in which I was shown two possible future lives, one in which I was part of a large, quite ordinary family and would devote myself to raising children and another where I was an only child. In this latter example I was born to an extremely loving and well-adjusted couple. It was clear that I would receive an abundance of love from them and would later feel happy and secure enough to live alone and offer myself in service to humanity. Quite unlike the 'me' who lives now, this individual was scientifically inclined. There was no question for me about which life I would choose even though I cannot imagine how it would be to have a brain capable of understanding physics and chemistry!

More recently I had a fascinating dream in which I was the Observer not only of my present life, but a past and future life too, all playing out in the same room of a house! It was a lucid dream – one in which I knew I was dreaming. My ex-husband was present and it was he who pointed out that a seated figure in the room was 'me' from a past life. I recognised her instantly, just as I 'recognised' the young girl, lying naked in bed, as 'me' in a future life. Our lives, past-present-future, cannot really be understood as sequential but viewed as all happening in the eternal now (just as my dream showed me), since on a wider scale Time does not exist.

In *Same Soul, Many Bodies*, Brian Weiss suggests that our future life conditions are always fluid since the future is created out of the very choices we make today. All this leads us to consider one of the most important Laws of Life: the Law of Cause and Effect or Karma. We all instinctively know the truth of this beautifully exact system that guarantees balance and justice. Just about everyone understands the phrase 'What goes around, comes around' without necessarily knowing about karma.
With each new life we have the opportunity to heal old issues of betrayal, selfishness and harm in our relationships with others so that we can eventually be free of karmic ties.

To conclude this section I would like to share a quotation from Henry Ford, founder of the Ford Motor Company, surprising because of the time it was written:

I adopted the theory of Reincarnation when I was twenty six. Religion offered nothing to the point. Even work could not give me complete satisfaction. Work is futile if we cannot utilise the experience we collect in one life in the next. When I discovered Reincarnation it was as if I had found a universal plan. I realised that there was a chance to work out my ideas. Time was no longer limited. I was no longer a slave to the hands of the clock. Genius is experience. Some seem to think that it is a gift or talent, but it is the fruit of long experience in many lives. Some are older souls than others, and so they know more. The discovery of Reincarnation put my mind at ease. If you preserve a record of this conversation, write it so that it puts men's minds at ease. I would like to communicate to others the calmness that the long view of life gives to us. Henry Ford (1928)

Interview in the San Francisco Examiner (26 August 1928)

Near Death Experiences
The current trend is, I believe, towards a more spiritually aware society. The rise in popularity of counselling; modern psychology; complementary healing, spiritualism and meditation are all signs of a mass awakening to our true identity as souls.

Many well-known doctors, including Elisabeth Kübler-Ross, Raymond Moody and Eben Alexander have described out of body and near-death phenomena. Some of the most interesting cases reported are those experienced by complete sceptics who, in extreme circumstances such as coma and even after being pronounced dead, suddenly find themselves 'out of body' but subsequently able to bring back seemingly impossible information. Neurosurgeon, Dr. Eben Alexander, is one such example. (See **Appendix:** *Proof of Heaven: A Neurosurgeon's Journey into the Afterlife*).

One story that particularly caught my eye was Dr Mary Neal's extraordinary account of her death. Although not a sceptic as such, Dr. Neal, an orthopedic surgeon, is a pragmatist and admits to having been previously hopeful but unsure of an afterlife. In 1999, she was kayaking with her husband and friends on a remote river in South America. While cascading down a waterfall, her kayak was dragged down and completely submerged. Despite the rescue efforts of her companions, Mary remained underwater too long and drowned. She describes the whole incident – how eventually she relaxed and felt no pain, how she was enveloped and held by a 'presence,' how she broke loose of the boat and found herself floating above the river. She was aware of the others in the canoeing party, all begging her to wake up, but at the same time was warmly greeted by ten or twelve 'spirits' and taken to a great hall. There was great celebration but they explained that it was not her time to die. She still had much to do, three things in particular: to protect her husband's health, to be a spiritual rock for the family after the (forthcoming) death of her eldest son, and to tell her story. She felt great sadness at having to leave that place but, having returned, both her life and her medical practice have been changed profoundly. Since her NDE she views herself as a healer rather than a surgeon. Even after her own son's predicted death she understands that he too will have felt no pain and will have been joyously greeted, just as she was. Her book, *To Heaven and Back* is the remarkable story of what happened as she moved from life to death to eternal life, and back again.

I had already collected a number of such reports and was interested in the possibility of gathering more medical evidence of survival. I was also aware that most members of the medical fraternity are unwilling to accept 'near death experiences' as anything more than symptoms of oxygen deprivation. But it's interesting, isn't it, how things come together at exactly the right time? Just as I'd committed to running *A Matter of Life and Death* an e-mail appeared in my Inbox, advertising a conference in London called 'Seeing through the Veil.' The list of speakers appealed to me: a Jungian analyst, a psychiatrist, a psychotherapist – and someone who'd had a Near Death Experience (NDE). I wasted no time and booked my place.

Two of the speakers had worked in NHS hospitals and clinics. Dr. Andrew Powell is a psychiatrist and psychotherapist whose interest in spirituality in healthcare led him to establish the Spirituality and Psychiatry Special

Interest Group in the Royal College of Psychiatrists. Encouragingly, this now has over 2500 psychiatrist members (2012).

In his talk, Andrew told of numbers of patients who, faced with Near Death Experiences, feel unable to discuss these with doctors. His view is that *psychiatry that affirms spiritual reality can help those who find themselves, sometimes to their consternation, 'seeing through the veil'.*

Psychotherapist Deborah Fish spoke of psycho-spiritual approaches to trauma and bereavement, using *Induced After-Death Communication* (IADC) together with *Eye Movement Desensitisation and Reprocessing* (EMDR). Deborah was trained by Dr. Allan Botkin and in 2012 was the only qualified IADC practitioner in the UK (see earlier section on **Mediumship, Eye Movement Therapy, and Induced After Death Communication**).

Jungian analyst, Anne Baring examined some current beliefs about death and suggested that the censorship any material related to 'non-ordinary' experiences limits the horizon of our sight. She also explored the approach to death in earlier cultures and the possible existence of a 'subtle' or 'light' body that offers us a very different understanding of our survival.

Despite my interest in the medical approach to NDEs the climax of the day was, for me, the appearance of the now well known author and speaker, Anita Moorjani. Her phenomenal near death experience is the subject of her book, 'Dying to be Me' (see **Appendix**). In 2002, Anita was diagnosed with cancer, which slowly spread throughout her body. By early 2006 her organs finally began to shut down and she went into a coma. The hospital doctors announced that she would not make it through the night.

At this point, although in a coma, she entered another dimension, while at the same time experiencing heightened awareness of everything that was taking place around her. During her experience she began to understand more fully her spiritual purpose here on earth and to realise why she had become ill in the first place. She had simply failed to 'be herself.' As she explained later: *Being yourself and being spiritual are one and the same thing.*

She was given a choice either to go further or to return to her present life. Were she to return she would, she was assured, regain full health.. Anita's choice to return subsequently led to a remarkable and complete recovery of her health.

Anita had previously tried every possible therapy, conventional and alternative, including strict dietary regimes in her search for a cure. Yet nothing had worked. She emphasised that no diet, however worthy, will ever be healing if we do not also enjoy our life – which may mean indulging in treats from time to time. (Later, over lunch, she caught me tucking into a rather delicious pudding - something I can rarely resist - and voiced her approval!).

Anita Moorjani's experience showed her the cause of her illness but also its antidote – the importance of living a meaningful, authentic and happy life.

The Last Five Minutes
So live your life that the fear of death can never enter your heart. Native American leader, Tecumseh

We began this chapter with the film that lent it its name and conclude with a reference to the film industry (for this I thank David Anderer, founder of the *Campaign for Beauty*). Apparently, there is a saying amongst film makers that the last five minutes can either make or break a movie. This is a useful metaphor to adopt, wherever we happen to be along the timeline of life. It also conveniently draws my attention to the end of my book.

Imagine your life as a film. To create a good ending you will need to look back at the whole story, a unique story created, acted, directed and now viewed – and reviewed - by you!

Now is your chance to weave together all your storylines, past and present, and make sense of the narrative so far. Here, in this 'last five minutes' you can resolve conflicts, end or mend relationships, create an unexpected turn of events or plot twist, reveal insights, fulfil dreams and even open doors for future adventures! It is an opportunity to find meaning in the challenges that befell you, the hero, and to inspire your audience (those who know you).

The 'last five minutes' is a real opportunity to draw on the resources of your Eternal Self and create the best possible conclusion to your life – however distant that conclusion may be.

Our spiritual life plays out in ordinary everyday things, as well as the extraordinary. That is what retreat 'whilst living and working in the world' teaches us. We are meant to experience life fully, not avoid worldly things. Remember too that your story affects humanity's story as a whole and how you live your life today creates memories for others as well as yourself. Although death is not The End, live each day as if it were your last; make each moment count and always strive to live beautifully, knowing that your life will echo through eternity ...

Fiery Love, **a sequel to this book, will be available in 2014**

APPENDIX

Useful Contacts, Resources and Recommended Reading

BEYOND DEATH AND DYING

The Tibetan Book of Living and Dying:
Sogyal Rinpoche (Rider)

Visions, Trips and Crowded Rooms: **David Kessler (Hay House)**

Dying to Be Me: **Anita Moorjani (Hay House)**

To Heaven and Back: **Dr. Mary Neal (WaterBrook Press)**

Far Journeys: **Robert Monroe (Broadway)**

Ultimate Journey: **Robert Monroe (Broadway)**

Many Lives, Many Masters: **Dr. Brian Weiss (Piatkus)**

Proof of Heaven: A Neurosurgeon's Journey into the Afterlife:
Dr. Eben Alexander (Piatkus)

Embraced by the Light (What happens when you die?):
Betty J. Eadie (Thorsons)

Ponder on This (section on Death and Dying):
(Lucis Trust Publishing)

INDUCED AFTER-DEATH COMMUNICATION

1. Dr. Allan Botkin
www.induced-adc.com

2. Deborah Mary Fish
www.deborahfish.com
Deborah is a psychotherapist and student of Dr. Botkin working in Birmingham, UK.

SITES FOR 'NON-ORDINARY' EXPERIENCES
(OBE's, NDE's, etc.)

Examples may be found on these and similar websites of phenomena such as NDE's and brain death; the blind able to see during NDE's; Scientific validation of NDE's and OBE's; Autoscopy (seeing one's own body from a distance) confirmed and validated; Scientific replication of OBE's; IADC (Moody and Zammit); NDE's and visions of the future; Group NDE's; Childhood experiences of NDE's; Life changing experience of NDE's; Consistency of details in NDE's; Scientific research into reincarnation and survival beyond death; Past-Life Regression; Contact with the deceased under scientific controls; Electronic Voice Phenomena; Prominent atheists experiencing NDE's.
www.near-death.com/experiences

University of Southampton research:
www.mikepettigrew.com/afterlife/html/ukstudy.html

http://www.childpastlives.org/birthmrk.htm

'A Lawyer Presents the Case for the Afterlife.' Since 2001 Victor Zammit, a retired lawyer, has placed on his website a sponsored one million dollars challenge to anyone who could show that the afterlife evidence is not valid. Mr. Zammit maintains that the burden of proof must be with the sceptics but many years later, no one has been able to beat the challenge. The million dollars sponsorship will apparently lapse in the year 2025.
http://www.victorzammit.com/book/chapter24.html
www.victorzammit.com

Dr. Andrew Powell
www.rcpsych.ac.uk/spirit

Dr. Mary Neal
www.drmaryneal.com

AGELESS WISDOM

When the Soul Awakens by Nancy Seifer and
Martin Vieweg
www.whenthesoulawakens.org

www.shareinternational.org
The Emergence of the World Teacher, solutions to our current global problems and Transmission Meditation Books by Benjamin Creme (highly recommended)

www.lucistrust.org
For information about, and excerpts from, books by Alice A. Bailey, and by the Master DK through Alice Bailey

www.agniyoga.org/aydownloads
For free downloads of books and letters by Helena Roerich who became a channel for the Master Morya. (It is said that Maitreya also gave information through her)

www.devorss.com
The Life and Teachings of the Masters of the Far East by Baird Spalding

SPIRITUAL PHILOSOPHY

www.jkrishnamurti.org
An on-line repository of books and video lectures by the great teacher, Jiddu Krishnamurti

Made in United States
Orlando, FL
24 April 2022

17135092R10111